Kaplan Publishing are constantly finding new
difference to your studies and our exciting on
offer something different to students looking

This book comes with free MyKaplan online re
study anytime, anywhere. **This free online re**
separately and is included in the price of the book.

Having purchased this book, you have access to the following online study materials:

CONTENT	ACCA (including FBT, FMA, FFA)		FIA (excluding FBT, FMA, FFA)	
	Text	Kit	Text	Kit
Electronic version of the book	✓	✓	✓	✓
Check Your Understanding Test with instant answers	✓			
Material updates	✓	✓	✓	✓
Latest official ACCA exam questions*		✓		
Extra question assistance using the signpost icon**		✓		
Timed questions with an online tutor debrief using clock icon***		✓		
Interim assessment including questions and answers	✓		✓	
Technical answers	✓	✓	✓	✓

* Excludes BT, MA, FA, FBT, FMA, FFA; for all other papers includes a selection of questions, as released by ACCA
** For ACCA SBL, SBR, AFM, APM, ATX, AAA only
*** Excludes BT, MA, FA, LW, FBT, FMA and FFA

How to access your online resources

Kaplan Financial students will already have a MyKaplan account and these extra resources will be available to you online. You do not need to register again, as this process was completed when you enrolled. If you are having problems accessing online materials, please ask your course administrator.

If you are not studying with Kaplan and did not purchase your book via a Kaplan website, to unlock your extra online resources please go to www.mykaplan.co.uk/addabook (even if you have set up an account and registered books previously). You will then need to enter the ISBN number (on the title page and back cover) and the unique pass key number contained in the scratch panel below to gain access. You will also be required to enter additional information during this process to set up or confirm your account details.

If you purchased through the Kaplan Publishing website you will automatically receive an e-mail invitation to MyKaplan. Please register your details using this email to gain access to your content. If you do not receive the e-mail or book content, please contact Kaplan Publishing.

Your Code and Information

This code can only be used once for the registration of one book online. This registration and your online content will expire when the final sittings for the examinations covered by this book have taken place. Please allow one hour from the time you submit your book details for us to process your request.

Please scratch the film to access your unique code.

Please be aware that this code is case-sensitive and you will need to include the dashes within the passcode, but not when entering the ISBN.

ACCA

Applied Knowledge

ACCA Diploma in Accounting and Business (RQF Level 4)

Management Accounting (MA/FMA)

Study Text

British library cataloguing-in-publication data

A catalogue record for this book is available from the British Library.

Published by:

Kaplan Publishing UK
Unit 2 The Business Centre
Molly Millars Lane
Wokingham
Berkshire
RG41 2QZ

ISBN 978-1-78740-855-5

Printed and bound in Great Britain

Acknowledgements

These materials are reviewed by the ACCA examining team. The objective of the review is to ensure that the material properly covers the syllabus and study guide outcomes, used by the examining team in setting the exams, in the appropriate breadth and depth. The review does not ensure that every eventuality, combination or application of examinable topics is addressed by the ACCA Approved Content. Nor does the review comprise a detailed technical check of the content as the Approved Content Provider has its own quality assurance processes in place in this respect.

We are grateful to the Association of Chartered Certified Accountants and the Chartered Institute of Management Accountants for permission to reproduce past examination questions. The answers have been prepared by Kaplan Publishing.

Contents

Introduction

How to use the Materials

These Kaplan Publishing learning materials have been carefully designed to make your learning experience as easy as possible and to give you the best chances of success in your examinations.

The product range contains a number of features to help you in the study process. They include:

(1) Detailed study guide and syllabus objectives

(2) Description of the examination

(3) Study skills and revision guidance

(4) Study text

(5) Question practice

The sections on the study guide, the syllabus objectives, the examination and study skills should all be read before you commence your studies. They are designed to familiarise you with the nature and content of the examination and give you tips on how to best to approach your learning.

The **Study Text** comprises the main learning materials and gives guidance as to the importance of topics and where other related resources can be found. Each chapter includes:

- The **learning objectives** contained in each chapter, which have been carefully mapped to the examining body's own syllabus learning objectives or outcomes. You should use these to check you have a clear understanding of all the topics on which you might be assessed in the examination.
- The **chapter diagram** provides a visual reference for the content in the chapter, giving an overview of the topics and how they link together.
- The **content** for each topic area commences with a brief explanation or definition to put the topic into context before covering the topic in detail. You should follow your studying of the content with a review of the illustration/s. These are worked examples which will help you to understand better how to apply the content for the topic.
- **Test your understanding** sections provide an opportunity to assess your understanding of the key topics by applying what you have learned to short questions. Answers can be found at the back of each chapter.
- **Summary diagrams** complete each chapter to show the important links between topics and the overall content of the examination. These diagrams should be used to check that you have covered and understood the core topics before moving on.
- **Question practice** is provided at the back of each text.

Quality and accuracy are of the utmost importance to us so if you spot an error in any of our products, please send an email to mykaplanreporting@kaplan.com with full details, or follow the link to the feedback form in MyKaplan.

Our Quality Coordinator will work with our technical team to verify the error and take action to ensure it is corrected in future editions.

Icon Explanations

Definition – Key definitions that you will need to learn from the core content.

Key point – Identifies topics that are key to success and are often examined.

Illustration – Worked examples help you understand the core content better.

Test your understanding – Exercises for you to complete to ensure that you have understood the topics just learned.

Supplementary reading – These sections will help to provide a deeper understanding of core areas. The supplementary reading is NOT optional reading. It is vital to provide you with the breadth of knowledge you will need to address the wide range of topics within your syllabus that could feature in an exam question. **Reference to this text is vital when self-studying.**

On-line subscribers

Our on-line resources are designed to increase the flexibility of your learning materials and provide you with immediate feedback on how your studies are progressing.

If you are subscribed to our on-line resources you will find:

(1) On-line reference ware: reproduces your Study Text on-line, giving you anytime, anywhere access.

(2) On-line testing: provides you with additional on-line objective testing so you can practice what you have learned further.

(3) On-line performance management: immediate access to your on-line testing results. Review your performance by key topics and chart your achievement through the course relative to your peer group.

Syllabus introduction

Syllabus background

The aim of ACCA **Management Accounting (MA)**/FIA Diploma in Accounting and Business is to develop knowledge and understanding of management accounting techniques to support management in planning, controlling and monitoring performance in a variety of business context.

Objectives of the syllabus

- Explain the nature, source and purpose of management information.
- Explain and analyse data analysis and statistical techniques.
- Explain and apply cost accounting techniques.
- Prepare budgets for planning and control.
- Compare actual costs with standard costs and analyse any variances.
- Explain and apply performance measurements and monitor business performance.

Core areas of the syllabus

- The nature, source and purpose of management information
- Data analysis and statistical techniques
- Cost accounting techniques
- Budgeting
- Standard costing
- Performance measurement.

ACCA Performance Objectives

In order to become a member of the ACCA, as a trainee accountant you will need to demonstrate that you have achieved nine performance objectives. Performance objectives are indicators of effective performance and set the minimum standard of work that trainees are expected to achieve and demonstrate in the workplace. They are divided into key areas of knowledge which are closely linked to the exam syllabus.

There are five Essential performance objectives and a choice of fifteen Technical performance objectives which are divided into five areas.

The performance objectives which link to this exam are:

(1) Ethics and professionalism PO1 (Essential)

(2) Evaluate management accounting systems PO12 (Technical)

(3) Plan and control performance PO13 (Technical)

(4) Monitor performance PO14 (Technical)

The following link provides an in depth insight into all of the performance objectives:

https://www.accaglobal.com/content/dam/ACCA_Global/Students/per/PER-Performance-objectives-achieve.pdf

Progression

There are two elements of progression that we can measure: first how quickly students move through individual topics within a subject; and second how quickly they move from one course to the next. We know that there is an optimum for both, but it can vary from subject to subject and from student to student. However, using data and our experience of student performance over many years, we can make some generalisations.

A fixed period of study set out at the start of a course with key milestones is important. This can be within a subject, for example 'I will finish this topic by 30 June', or for overall achievement, such as 'I want to be qualified by the end of next year'.

Your qualification is cumulative, as earlier papers provide a foundation for your subsequent studies, so do not allow there to be too big a gap between one subject and another. We know that exams encourage techniques that lead to some degree of short term retention, the result being that you will simply forget much of what you have already learned unless it is refreshed (look up Ebbinghaus Forgetting Curve for more details on this). This makes it more difficult as you move from one subject to another: not only will you have to learn the new subject, you will also have to relearn all the underpinning knowledge as well. This is very inefficient and slows down your overall progression which makes it more likely you may not succeed at all.

In addition, delaying your studies slows your path to qualification which can have negative impacts on your career, postponing the opportunity to apply for higher level positions and therefore higher pay.

You can use the following diagram showing the whole structure of your qualification to help you keep track of your progress.

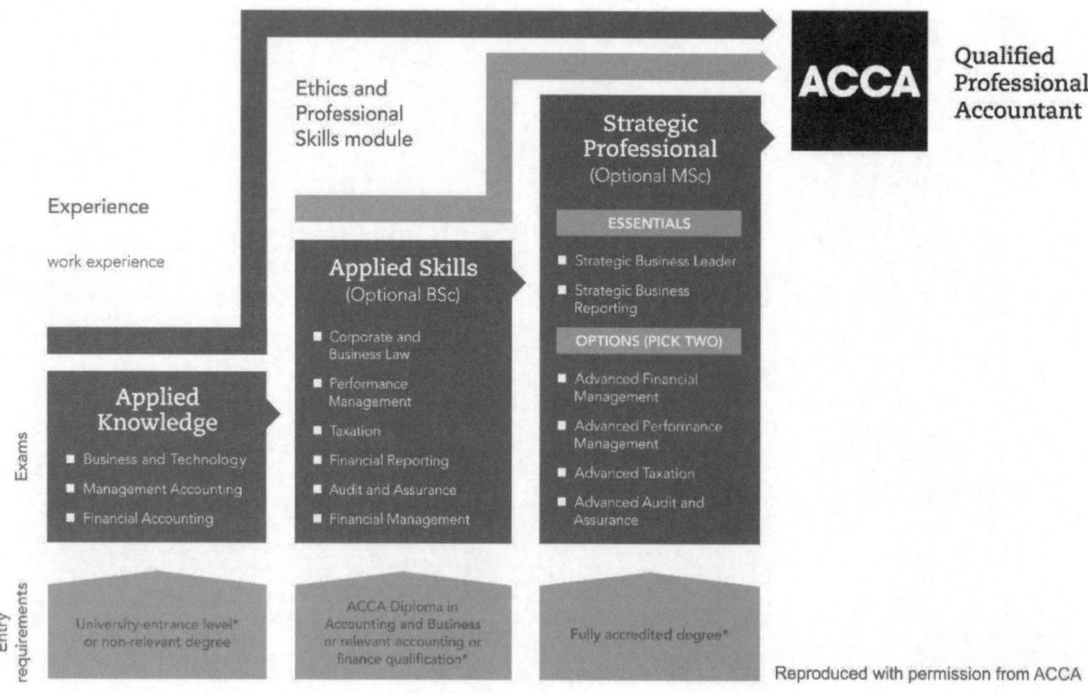

Reproduced with permission from ACCA

Syllabus objectives

We have reproduced the ACCA's syllabus below, showing where the objectives are explored within this book. Within the chapters, we have broken down the extensive information found in the syllabus into easily digestible and relevant sections, called Content Objectives. These correspond to the objectives at the beginning of each chapter.

Syllabus learning objective			Chapter reference
A	**THE NATURE, SOURCE AND PURPOSE OF MANAGEMENT INFORMATION**		
1	**Accounting for management**		
	(a)	Describe the purpose and role of cost and management accounting within an organisation.[k]	1
	(b)	Compare and contrast financial accounting with cost and management accounting.[k]	1
	(c)	Outline the managerial processes of planning, decision making and control.[k]	1
	(d)	Explain the difference between strategic, tactical and operational planning.[k]	1
	(e)	Distinguish between data and information.[k]	1
	(f)	Identify and explain the attributes of good information.[k]	1
	(g)	Explain the limitations of management information in providing guidance for managerial decision-making.[k]	1
2	**Sources of data**		
	(a)	Describe the three main data sources: machine/sensor, transactional and human/social [k]	10
	(b)	Describe sources of information from within and outside the organisation (including government statistics, financial press, professional or trade associations, quotations and price list).[k]	10
	(c)	Explain the uses and limitations of published information/data (including information from the internet).[k]	10
	(d)	Describe the impact of general economic environment on costs/revenues.[k]	10

3 Cost classification

(a)	Explain and illustrate production and non-production costs.[k]	2
(b)	Describe the different elements of non-production costs – administrative, selling, distribution and finance.[k]	2
(c)	Describe the different elements of production cost – materials, labour and overheads.[k]	2
(d)	Explain the importance of the distinction between production and non-production costs when valuing output and inventories.[k]	2
(e)	Explain and illustrate with examples classifications used in the analysis of the product/service costs including by function, direct and indirect, fixed and variable, stepped fixed and semi variable costs.[s]	2
(f)	Explain and illustrate the use of codes in categorising transaction.[k]	2
(g)	Describe and illustrate, graphically, different types of cost behaviour.[s]	2
(h)	Explain and illustrate the concept of cost objects, cost units and cost centres.[s]	2
(i)	Distinguish between cost, profit, investment and revenue centres.[k]	1
(j)	Describe the differing needs for information of cost, profit, investment and revenue centre managers.[k]	1

4 Presenting information

(a)	Prepare written reports representing management information in suitable formats according to purpose.[s]	17
(b)	Present information using table, charts and graphs (bar charts, line graphs, pie charts and scatter graphs).[s]	17
(c)	Interpret information (including the above tables, charts and graphs) presented in management reports.[s]	17

B DATA ANALYSIS AND STATISTICAL TECHNIQUES

1 Sampling methods

(a) Explain sampling techniques (random, systematic, stratified, multistage, cluster and quota).[k] 10

(b) Choose an appropriate sampling method in a specific situation. (Note: Derivation of random samples will not be examined).[s] 10

2 Forecasting techniques

(a) Explain the structure of linear functions and equations.[s] 2

(b) Use high/low analysis to separate the fixed and variable elements of total costs including situations involving semi variable and stepped fixed costs and changes in the variable cost per unit.[s] 2

(c) Explain the advantages and disadvantages of using high low method to estimate the fixed and variable element of costing.[k] 2

(d) Construct scatter diagrams and lines of best fit.[s] 17

(e) Analysis of cost data. 12

- (i) Explain the concept of correlation coefficient and coefficient of determination.[k] 12
- (ii) Calculate and interpret correlation coefficient and coefficient of determination.[s] 12
- (iii) Establish a linear function using regression analysis and interpret the results.[s] 12

(f) Use liner regression coefficients to make forecasts of costs and revenues.[s] 12

(g) Adjust historical and forecast data for price movements.[s] 12

(h) Explain the advantages and disadvantages of linear regression analysis.[k] 12

(i) Explain the principles of time series analysis (cyclical, trend, seasonal variation and random elements).[k] 12

(j) Calculate moving averages.[s] 12

(k) Calculation of trend, including the use of regression coefficients.[s] 12

(l) Use trend and seasonal variation (additive and multiplicative) to make budget forecasts.[s] 12

(m) Explain the advantages and disadvantages of time series analysis.[k] 12

(n) Explain the purpose of index numbers.[k] 12

	(o)	Calculate simple and multi-item (weighted) index numbers for one or more variables, including Laspeyre and Paasche indicies.[s]	12
	(p)	Describe the product life cycle and explain its importance in forecasting.[k]	12
3	**Summarising and analysing data**		
	(a)	Describe the five characteristics of big data (volume, variety, velocity, value and veracity).[k]	10
	(b)	Explain the three types of big data: structured, semi-structured and unstructured.[k]	10
	(c)	Describe the main uses of big data and analytics for organisations.[k]	10
	(d)	Describe the two types of data categorical (nominal and ordinal) and numerical (continuous and discrete).[s]	10
	(e)	Explain the terms descriptive analysis and inferential analysis.[k]	10
	(f)	Calculate the mean, mode and median for ungrouped data and the mean for grouped data.[s]	11
	(g)	Calculate measures of dispersion including the variance, standard deviation and coefficient of variation both grouped and ungrouped data.[s]	11
	(h)	Calculate expected values for use in decision-making.[s]	11
	(i)	Explain the properties of a normal distribution.[s]	11
	(j)	Interpret normal distribution graphs and tables.[s]	11
4	**Spreadsheets**		
	(a)	Explain the role and features of a computer spreadsheet system.[k]	18
	(b)	Identify applications for computer spreadsheets and their use in cost and management accounting.[s]	18

C COST ACCOUNTING TECHNIQUES

1 Accounting for material, labour and overheads

(a) Accounting for materials

(i)	Describe the different procedures and documents necessary for the ordering, receiving and issuing of materials from inventory.[k]	3
(ii)	Describe the control procedures used to monitor physical and 'book' inventory and to minimise discrepancies and losses.[k]	3
(iii)	Interpret the entries and balances in the material inventory account.[s]	3
(iv)	Identify, explain and calculate the costs of ordering and holding inventory (including buffer inventory).[s]	3
(v)	Calculate and interpret optimal reorder quantities.[s]	3
(vi)	Calculate and interpret optimal reorder quantities when discounts apply.[s]	3
(vii)	Produce calculations to minimise inventory costs when inventory is gradually replenished.[s]	3
(viii)	Describe and apply appropriate methods for establishing reorder levels where demand in the lead time is constant.[s]	3
(ix)	Calculate the value of closing inventory and material issues using LIFO, FIFO and average methods.[s]	3

(b) Accounting for labour

(i)	Calculate direct and indirect costs of labour.[s]	4
(ii)	Explain the methods used to relate input labour costs to work done.[k]	4
(iii)	Prepare the journal and ledger entries to record labour cost inputs and outputs.[s]	4
(iv)	Describe different remuneration methods: time-based systems, piecework systems and individual and group incentive schemes.[k]	4
(v)	Calculate the level, and analyse the costs and causes of labour turnover.[s]	4
(vi)	Explain and calculate labour efficiency, capacity and production volume ratios.[s]	4
(vii)	Interpret the entries in the labour account.[s]	4

(c) Accounting for overheads

(i) Explain the different treatment of direct and indirect expenses.[k] 5

(ii) Describe the procedures involved in determining production overhead absorption rates.[k] 5

(iii) Allocate and apportion production overheads to cost centres using an appropriate basis.[s] 5

(iv) Reapportion service cost centre costs to production cost centres (including using the reciprocal method where service cost centres work for each other).[s] 5

(v) Select, apply and discuss appropriate bases for absorption rates.[s] 5

(vi) Prepare journal and ledger entries for manufacturing overheads incurred and absorbed.[s] 5

(vii) Calculate and explain the under and over absorption of overheads.[s] 5

2 Absorption and marginal costing

(a) Explain the importance of, and apply, the concept of contribution.[s] 6

(b) Demonstrate and discuss the effect of absorption and marginal costing on inventory valuation and profit determination.[s] 6

(c) Calculate profit or loss under absorption and marginal costing.[s] 6

(d) Reconcile the profits or losses calculated under absorption and marginal costing.[s] 6

(e) Describe the advantages and disadvantages of absorption and marginal costing.[k] 6

3 Cost accounting methods

(a) Job and batch costing

(i) Describe the characteristics of job and batch costing.[k] 7

(ii) Describe the situations where the use of job or batch costing would be appropriate.[k] 7

(iii) Prepare cost records and accounts in job and batch costing situations.[k] 7

(iv) Establish job and batch costs from given information.[s] 7

(b) Process costing

(i)	Describe the characteristics of process costing.[k]	7
(ii)	Describe the situations where the use of process costing would be appropriate.[s]	7
(iii)	Explain the concepts of normal and abnormal losses and abnormal gains.[k]	7
(iv)	Calculate the cost per unit of process outputs.[s]	7
(v)	Prepare process accounts involving normal and abnormal losses and abnormal gains.[s]	7
(vi)	Calculate and explain the concept of equivalent units.[s]	7
(vii)	Apportion process costs between work remaining in process and transfers out of a process using the weighted average and FIFO methods.[s]	7
(viii)	Prepare process accounts in situations where work remains incomplete.[s]	7
(ix)	Prepare process accounts where losses and gains are identified at different stages of the process.[s]	7
(x)	Distinguish between by-products and joint products.[k]	7
(xi)	Value by-products and joint products at the point of separation.[s]	7
(xii)	Prepare process accounts in situations where by-products and/or joint products occur.[s]	7

Note: Situations involving work in process and losses in the same process are excluded.

(c) Service/operation costing

(i)	Identify situations where the use of service/operation costing is appropriate.[k]	8
(ii)	Illustrate suitable unit cost measures that may be used in different service/operation situations.[s]	8
(iii)	Carry out service cost analysis in simple service industry situations.[s]	8

4	**Alternative costing principles**		
	(a)	Explain activity based costing (ABC), target costing, life cycle costing and total quality management (TQM) as alternative cost management techniques.[k]	9
	(b)	Differentiate ABC, target costing and life cycle costing from the traditional costing techniques (note: calculations are not required).[k]	9
D	**BUDGETING**		
1	**Nature and purpose of budgeting**		
	(a)	Explain why organisations use budgeting.[k]	13
	(b)	Describe the planning and control cycle in an organisation.[k]	13
	(c)	Explain the administrative procedures used in the budgeting process.[k]	13
	(d)	Describe the stages in the budgeting process (including sources of relevant data, planning and agreeing draft budgets and purpose of forecasting and how they link to budgeting).[k]	13
2	**Budget preparation**		
	(a)	Explain the importance of principal budget factor in constructing the budget.[k]	13
	(b)	Prepare sales budgets.[s]	13
	(c)	Prepare functional budgets (production, raw materials usage and purchases, labour, variable and fixed overheads).[s]	13
	(d)	Prepare cash budgets.[s]	13
	(e)	Prepare master budgets (statement of profit and loss and statement of financial position).[s]	13
	(f)	Explain and illustrate 'what if' analysis and scenario planning.[s]	13
3	**Flexible budgets**		
	(a)	Explain the importance of flexible budgets in control.[k]	13
	(b)	Explain the disadvantage of fixed budgets in control.[k]	13
	(c)	Identify situations where fixed or flexible budgetary control would be appropriate.[k]	13
	(d)	Flex a budget to a given level of volume.[s]	13

4 Capital budgeting and discounted cash flows

(a)	Discuss the importance of capital investment and planning and control.[k]	14
(b)	Define and distinguish between capital and revenue expenditure.[k]	14
(c)	Outline the issues to consider and the steps involved in the preparation of a capital expenditure budget.[k]	14
(d)	Explain and illustrate the difference between simple and compound interest, and between nominal and effective interest rates.[s]	14
(e)	Explain and illustrate compounding and discounting.[s]	14
(f)	Explain the distinction between cash flow and profit and the relevance of cash flow to capital investment appraisal.[k]	14
(g)	Identify and evaluate relevant cash flows for individual investment decisions.[s]	14
(h)	Explain and illustrate the net present value (NPV) and internal rate of return (IRR) methods of discounted cash flow.[s]	14
(i)	Calculate present value using annuity and perpetuity formulae.[s]	14
(j)	Calculate NPV, IRR and payback (discounted and non-discounted).[s]	14
(k)	Interpret the results of NPV, IRR and payback calculations of investment viability.[s]	14

5 Budgetary control and reporting

(a)	Calculate simple variances between flexed budget, fixed budget and actual sales, costs and profits.[s]	13
(b)	Discuss the relative significance of variances.[k]	15
(c)	Explain potential action to eliminate variances.[k]	15
(d)	Define the concept of responsibility accounting and its significance in control.[k]	13
(e)	Explain the concept of controllable and uncontrollable costs.[k]	13
(f)	Prepare control reports suitable for presentation to management (to include recommendation of appropriate control action).[s]	13

6 Behavioural aspects of budgeting

(a)	Explain the importance of motivation in performance management.[k]	13
(b)	Identify factors in a budgetary planning and control system that influence motivation.[k]	13
(c)	Explain the impact of targets upon motivation.[k]	13
(d)	Discuss managerial incentive schemes.[k]	13
(e)	Discuss the advantages and disadvantages of a participative approach to budgeting.[k]	13
(f)	Explain top down, bottom up approaches to budgeting.[k]	13

E STANDARD COSTING

1 Standard costing systems

(a)	Explain the purpose and principles of standard costing.[k]	15
(b)	Explain the difference between standard, marginal and absorption costing.[k]	15
(c)	Establish the standard cost per unit under absorption and marginal costing.[k]	15

2 Variance calculations and analysis

(a)	Calculate sales price and volume variance.[s]	15
(b)	Calculate materials total, price and usage variance.[s]	15
(c)	Calculate labour total, rate and efficiency variance.[s]	15
(d)	Calculate variable overhead total, expenditure and efficiency.[s]	15
(e)	Calculate fixed overhead total, expenditure and, where appropriate, volume, capacity and efficiency.[s]	15
(f)	Interpret the variances.[s]	15
(g)	Explain factors to consider before investigating variances, explain possible causes of the variances and recommend control action.[s]	15
(h)	Explain the interrelationships between the variances.[k]	15
(i)	Calculate actual or standard figures where the variances are given.[k]	15

3	**Reconciliation of budgeted profit and actual profit**		
	(a)	Reconcile budgeted profit with actual profit under standard absorption costing.[s]	15
	(b)	Reconcile budgeted profit or contribution with actual profit or contribution under standard marginal costing.[s]	15
F	**PERFORMANCE MEASUREMENT**		
1	**Performance measurement overview**		
	(a)	Discuss the purpose of mission statements and their role in performance measurement.[k]	16
	(b)	Discuss the purpose of strategic and operational and tactical objectives and their role in performance measurement.[k]	16
	(c)	Discuss the impact of economic and market condition on performance measurement.[k]	16
	(d)	Explain the impact of government regulation on performance measurement.[k]	16
2	**Performance measurement – application**		
	(a)	Discuss and calculate measures of financial performance (profitability, liquidity, activity and gearing) and non-financial measures.[s]	16
	(b)	Perspectives of the balance scorecard.	16
		(i) Discuss the advantages and limitations of the balance scorecard.[k]	16
		(ii) Describe performance indicators for financial, customer, internal business process and innovation and learning.[k]	16
		(iii) Discuss critical success factors and key performance indicators and their link to objectives and mission statements.[k]	16
		(iv) Establish critical success factors and key performance indicators in a specific situation.[s]	16
	(c)	Economy, efficiency and effectiveness	16
		(i) Explain the concepts of economy, efficiency and effectiveness.[k]	16
		(ii) Describe performance indicators for economy, efficiency and effectiveness.[k]	16
		(iii) Establish performance indicators for economy, efficient and effectiveness in a specific situation.[s]	16
		(iv) Discuss the meaning of each of the efficiency, capacity and activity ratios.[k]	16
		(v) Calculate the efficiency, capacity and activity ratios in a specific situation.[s]	16

(d) Unit costs 16

(i) Describe performance measures which would be suitable in contract and process costing environments.[k]

(e) Resources utilisation

(i) Describe measures of performance utilisation in service and manufacturing environments.[k] 16

(ii) Establish measures of resource utilisation in a specific situation.[s] 16

(f) Profitability

(i) Calculate return on investment and residual income.[s] 16

(ii) Explain the advantages and limitations of return on investment and residual income.[k] 16

(g) Quality of service 16

(i) Distinguish performance measurement issues in service and manufacturing industries.[k] 16

(ii) Describe performance measures appropriate for service industries.[k] 16

3 Cost reductions and value enhancement

(a) Compare cost control and cost reduction.[s] 16

(b) Describe and evaluate cost reduction methods.[s] 16

(c) Describe and evaluate value analysis.[s] 16

4 Monitoring performance and reporting

(a) Discuss the importance of non-financial performance measures.[k] 16

(b) Discuss the relationship between short-term and long-term performance.[k] 16

(c) Discuss the measurement of performance in service industry situations.[k] 16

(d) Discuss the measurement of performance in non-profit seeking and public sector organisations.[k] 16

(e) Discuss measures that may be used to assess managerial performance and the practical problems involved.[k] 16

(f) Discuss the role of benchmarking in performance measurement.[k] 16

(g) Produce reports highlighting key areas for management attention and recommendations for improvement.[k] 16

The examination

Examination format

The syllabus is assessed by a two-hour computer-based examination. Questions will assess all parts of the syllabus and will contain both computational and non-computational elements:

	Number of marks
Section A 35 two mark objective questions	70
Section B 3 ten mark multi-task questions	30
	100

Section B will examine Budgeting, Standard costing and Performance measurement. Note: Budgeting MTQs in Section B can also include tasks from syllabus area B2 Forecasting techniques. B4 Spreadsheets could be included in any of the MTQs, as either the basis for the presentation of information in the question scenario or as a task within the MTQ.

Total time allowed: 2 hours

Examination tips

Spend the first few minutes of the examination reviewing the format and content so that you understand what you need to do.

Divide the time you spend on questions in proportion to the marks on offer. One suggestion for **this exam** is to allocate 1 minutes and 12 seconds to each mark available, so each 2-mark question should be completed in 2 minutes 24 seconds or approximately 2 and a half minutes.

Computer-based examination (CBE) tips

Be sure you understand how to use the software before you start the exam. If in doubt, ask the assessment centre staff to explain it to you.

Questions are **displayed on the screen** and answers are entered using keyboard and mouse. At the end of the exam, you are given a certificate showing the result you have achieved.

Do not attempt a CBE until you have **completed all study material** relating to it. **Do not skip any of the material** in the syllabus.

Read each question very carefully.

Double-check your answer before committing yourself to it.

Answer every question – if you do not know an answer, you don't lose anything by guessing. Think carefully before you **guess**.

The CBE question types are as follows:

- Multiple choice – where you are required to choose one answer from a list of options provided by clicking on the appropriate 'radio button'
- Multiple response – where you are required to select more than one response from the options provided by clicking on the appropriate tick boxes(typically choose two options from the available list
- Multiple response matching – where you are required to indicate a response to a number of related statements by clicking on the 'radio button' which corresponds to the appropriate response for each statement
- Number entry – where you are required to key in a response to a question shown on the screen.

With an objective test question, it may be possible to eliminate first those answers that you know are wrong. Then choose the most appropriate answer(s) as required from those that are left. This could be a single answer (e.g. multiple choice) or more than one response (e.g. multiple response and multiple response – matching).

After you have eliminated the ones that you know to be wrong, if you are still unsure, guess. But only do so after you have double-checked that you have only eliminated answers that are definitely wrong.

Don't panic if you realise you've answered a question incorrectly. Getting one question wrong will not mean the difference between passing and failing.

ACCA Support

For additional support with your studies please also refer to the ACCA Global website.

Study skills and revision guidance

This section aims to give guidance on how to study for your ACCA exams and to give ideas on how to improve your existing study techniques.

Preparing to study

Set your objectives

Before starting to study decide what you want to achieve – the type of pass you wish to obtain. This will decide the level of commitment and time you need to dedicate to your studies.

Devise a study plan

Determine which times of the week you will study.

Split these times into sessions of at least one hour for study of new material. Any shorter periods could be used for revision or practice.

Put the times you plan to study onto a study plan for the weeks from now until the exam and set yourself targets for each period of study – in your sessions make sure you cover the course, course assignments and revision.

If you are studying for more than one examination at a time, try to vary your subjects as this can help you to keep interested and see subjects as part of wider knowledge.

When working through your course, compare your progress with your plan and, if necessary, re-plan your work (perhaps including extra

Effective studying

Active reading

You are not expected to learn the text by rote, rather, you must understand what you are reading and be able to use it to pass the exam and develop good practice. A good technique to use is SQ3Rs – Survey, Question, Read, Recall, Review:

(1) **Survey the chapter** – look at the headings and read the introduction, summary and objectives, so as to get an overview of what the chapter deals with.

(2) **Question** – whilst undertaking the survey, ask yourself the questions that you hope the chapter will answer for you.

(3) **Read** through the chapter thoroughly, answering the questions and making sure you can meet the objectives. Attempt the exercises and activities in the text, and work through all the examples.

(4) **Recall** – at the end of each section and at the end of the chapter, try to recall the main ideas of the section/chapter without referring to the text. This is best done after a short break of a couple of minutes after the reading stage.

(5) **Review** – check that your recall notes are correct.

You may also find it helpful to re-read the chapter to try to see the topic(s) it deals with as a whole.

Note-taking

Taking notes is a useful way of learning, but do not simply copy out the text. The notes must:

- be in your own words
- be concise
- cover the key points
- be well-organised
- be modified as you study further chapters in this text or in related ones.

Trying to summarise a chapter without referring to the text can be a useful way of determining which areas you know and which you don't.

Three ways of taking notes:

Summarise the key points of a chapter.

Make linear notes – a list of headings, divided up with subheadings listing the key points. If you use linear notes, you can use different colours to highlight key points and keep topic areas together. Use plenty of space to make your notes easy to use.

Try a diagrammatic form – the most common of which is a mind-map. To make a mind-map, put the main heading in the centre of the paper and put a circle around it. Then draw short lines radiating from this to the main sub-headings, which again have circles around them. Then continue the process from the sub-headings to sub-sub-headings, advantages, disadvantages, etc.

Highlighting and underlining

You may find it useful to underline or highlight key points in your study text – but do be selective. You may also wish to make notes in the margins.

Revision

The best approach to revision is to revise the course as you work through it. Also try to leave four to six weeks before the exam for final revision. Make sure you cover the whole syllabus and pay special attention to those areas where your knowledge is weak. Here are some recommendations:

Read through the text and your notes again and condense your notes into key phrases. It may help to put key revision points onto index cards to look at when you have a few minutes to spare.

Review any assignments you have completed and look at where you lost marks – put more work into those areas where you were weak.

Practise exam standard questions under timed conditions. If you are short of time, list the points you would include or specify the calculations that you would include in your answer and then read the model answer, but do try to complete at least a few questions under exam conditions.

If you are stuck on a topic find somebody (e.g. your tutor or, where appropriate, a member of Kaplan's Academic Support team) to explain it to you

Read good newspapers and professional journals, especially ACCA's Student Accountant – this can give you an advantage in the exam.

Ensure you **know the structure of the exam** – how many questions and of what type you will be expected to answer. During your revision attempt all the different styles of questions you may be asked.

Further reading

You can find further reading and technical articles under the student section of ACCA's website.

Technical update

This text has been updated to reflect Examinable Documents September 2021 to August 2022 issued by ACCA

FORMULAE AND TABLES

Regression analysis

$$y = a + bx$$

$$a = \frac{\sum y}{n} - \frac{b\sum x}{n}$$

$$b = \frac{n\sum xy - \sum x \sum y}{n\sum x^2 - (\sum x)^2}$$

$$r = \frac{n\sum xy - \sum x \sum y}{\sqrt{(n\sum x^2 - (\sum x)^2)(n\sum y^2 - (\sum y)^2)}}$$

Economic order quantity

$$= \sqrt{\frac{2C_0D}{C_h}}$$

Economic batch quantity

$$= \sqrt{\frac{2C_0D}{C_h\left(1 - \frac{D}{R}\right)}}$$

Arithmetic mean

$$\bar{x} = \frac{\Sigma x}{n} \qquad \bar{x} = \frac{\Sigma fx}{\Sigma f} \text{ (frequency distribution)}$$

Standard deviation

$$\sigma = \sqrt{\frac{\Sigma(x - \bar{x})^2}{n}} \qquad \sigma = \sqrt{\frac{\Sigma fx^2}{\Sigma f} - \left(\frac{\Sigma fx}{\Sigma f}\right)^2} \text{ (frequency distribution)}$$

Variance

$$= \sigma^2$$

Co-efficient of variation

$$CV = \frac{\sigma}{\bar{x}}$$

Expected value

$$EV = \sum px$$

Present value table

Present value of 1, i.e. $(1 + r)^{-n}$

Where r = discount rate

n = number of periods until payment

Periods	Discount rate (r)									
(n)	1%	2%	3%	4%	5%	6%	7%	8%	9%	10%
1	0.990	0.980	0.971	0.962	0.952	0.943	0.935	0.926	0.917	0.909
2	0.980	0.961	0.943	0.925	0.907	0.890	0.873	0.857	0.842	0.826
3	0.971	0.942	0.915	0.889	0.864	0.840	0.816	0.794	0.772	0.751
4	0.961	0.924	0.888	0.855	0.823	0.792	0.763	0.735	0.708	0.683
5	0.951	0.906	0.863	0.822	0.784	0.747	0.713	0.681	0.650	0.621
6	0.942	0.888	0.837	0.790	0.746	0.705	0.666	0.630	0.596	0.564
7	0.933	0.871	0.813	0.760	0.711	0.665	0.623	0.583	0.547	0.513
8	0.923	0.853	0.789	0.731	0.677	0.627	0.582	0.540	0.502	0.467
9	0.914	0.837	0.766	0.703	0.645	0.592	0.544	0.500	0.460	0.424
10	0.905	0.820	0.744	0.676	0.614	0.558	0.508	0.463	0.422	0.386
11	0.896	0.804	0.722	0.650	0.585	0.527	0.475	0.429	0.388	0.350
12	0.887	0.788	0.701	0.625	0.557	0.497	0.444	0.397	0.356	0.319
13	0.879	0.773	0.681	0.601	0.530	0.469	0.415	0.368	0.326	0.290
14	0.870	0.758	0.661	0.577	0.505	0.442	0.388	0.340	0.299	0.263
15	0.861	0.743	0.642	0.555	0.481	0.417	0.362	0.315	0.275	0.239

(n)	11%	12%	13%	14%	15%	16%	17%	18%	19%	20%
1	0.901	0.893	0.885	0.877	0.870	0.862	0.855	0.847	0.840	0.833
2	0.812	0.797	0.783	0.769	0.756	0.743	0.731	0.718	0.706	0.694
3	0.731	0.712	0.693	0.675	0.658	0.641	0.624	0.609	0.593	0.579
4	0.659	0.636	0.613	0.592	0.572	0.552	0.534	0.516	0.499	0.482
5	0.593	0.567	0.543	0.519	0.497	0.476	0.456	0.437	0.419	0.402
6	0.535	0.507	0.480	0.456	0.432	0.410	0.390	0.370	0.352	0.335
7	0.482	0.452	0.425	0.400	0.376	0.354	0.333	0.314	0.296	0.279
8	0.434	0.404	0.376	0.351	0.327	0.305	0.285	0.266	0.249	0.233
9	0.391	0.361	0.333	0.308	0.284	0.263	0.243	0.225	0.209	0.194
10	0.352	0.322	0.295	0.270	0.247	0.227	0.208	0.191	0.176	0.162
11	0.317	0.287	0.261	0.237	0.215	0.195	0.178	0.162	0.148	0.135
12	0.286	0.257	0.231	0.208	0.187	0.168	0.152	0.137	0.124	0.112
13	0.258	0.229	0.204	0.182	0.163	0.145	0.130	0.116	0.104	0.093
14	0.232	0.205	0.181	0.160	0.141	0.125	0.111	0.099	0.088	0.078
15	0.209	0.183	0.160	0.140	0.123	0.108	0.095	0.084	0.074	0.065

Annuity table

Present value of an annuity of 1, i.e. $\frac{1-(1+r)^{-n}}{r}$

Where r = discount rate

n = number of periods

Periods (n)	Discount rate (r) 1%	2%	3%	4%	5%	6%	7%	8%	9%	10%
1	0.990	0.980	0.971	0.962	0.952	0.943	0.935	0.926	0.917	0.909
2	1.970	1.942	1.913	1.886	1.859	1.833	1.808	1.783	1.759	1.736
3	2.941	2.884	2.829	2.775	2.723	2.673	2.624	2.577	2.531	2.487
4	3.902	3.808	3.717	3.630	3.546	3.465	3.387	3.312	3.240	3.170
5	4.853	4.713	4.580	4.452	4.329	4.212	4.100	3.993	3.890	3.791
6	5.795	5.601	5.417	5.242	5.076	4.917	4.767	4.623	4.486	4.355
7	6.728	6.472	6.230	6.002	5.786	5.582	5.389	5.206	5.033	4.868
8	7.652	7.325	7.020	6.733	6.463	6.210	5.971	5.747	5.535	5.335
9	8.566	8.162	7.786	7.435	7.108	6.802	6.515	6.247	5.995	5.759
10	9.471	8.983	8.530	8.111	7.722	7.360	7.024	6.710	6.418	6.145
11	10.368	9.787	9.253	8.760	8.306	7.887	7.499	7.139	6.805	8.495
12	11.255	10.575	9.954	9.385	8.863	8.384	7.943	7.536	7.161	6.814
13	12.134	11.348	10.635	9.986	9.394	8.853	8.358	7.904	7.487	7.103
14	13.004	12.106	11.296	10.563	9.899	9.295	8.745	8.244	7.786	7.367
15	13.865	12.849	11.938	11.118	10.380	9.712	9.108	8.559	8.061	7.606

(n)	11%	12%	13%	14%	15%	16%	17%	18%	19%	20%
1	0.901	0.893	0.885	0.877	0.870	0.862	0.855	0.847	0.840	0.833
2	1.713	1.690	1.668	1.647	1.626	1.605	1.585	1.566	1.547	1.528
3	2.444	2.402	2.361	2.322	2.283	2.246	2.210	2.174	2.140	2.106
4	3.102	3.037	2.974	2.914	2.855	2.798	2.743	2.690	2.639	2.589
5	3.696	3.605	3.517	3.433	3.352	3.274	3.199	3.127	3.058	2.991
6	4.231	4.111	3.998	3.889	3.784	3.685	3.589	3.498	3.410	3.326
7	4.712	4.564	4.423	4.288	4.160	4.039	3.922	3.812	3.706	3.605
8	5.146	4.968	4.799	4.639	4.487	4.344	4.207	4.078	3.954	3.837
9	5.537	5.328	5.132	4.946	4.772	4.607	4.451	4.303	4.163	4.031
10	5.889	5.650	5.426	5.216	5.019	4.833	4.659	4.494	4.339	4.192
11	6.207	5.938	5.687	5.453	5.234	5.029	4.836	4.656	4.486	4.327
12	6.492	6.194	5.918	5.660	5.421	5.197	4.968	4.793	4.611	4.439
13	6.750	6.424	6.122	5.842	5.583	5.342	5.118	4.910	4.715	4.533
14	6.982	6.628	6.302	6.002	5.724	5.468	5.229	5.008	4.802	4.611
15	7.191	6.811	6.462	6.142	5.847	5.575	5.324	5.092	4.876	4.675

Standard normal distribution table

$$z = \frac{x - \mu}{\sigma}$$

	0.00	0.01	0.02	0.03	0.04	0.05	0.06	0.07	0.08	0.09
0.0	0.0000	0.0040	0.0080	0.0120	0.0160	0.0199	0.0239	0.0279	0.0319	0.0359
0.1	0.0398	0.0438	0.0478	0.0517	0.0557	0.0596	0.0636	0.0675	0.0714	0.0753
0.2	0.0793	0.0832	0.0871	0.0910	0.0948	0.0987	0.1026	0.1064	0.1103	0.1141
0.3	0.1179	0.1217	0.1255	0.1293	0.1331	0.1368	0.1406	0.1443	0.1480	0.1517
0.4	0.1554	0.1591	0.1628	0.1664	0.1700	0.1736	0.1772	0.1808	0.1844	0.1879
0.5	0.1915	0.1950	0.1985	0.2019	0.2054	0.2088	0.2123	0.2157	0.2190	0.2224
0.6	0.2257	0.2291	0.2324	0.2357	0.2389	0.2422	0.2454	0.2486	0.2517	0.2549
0.7	0.2580	0.2611	0.2642	0.2673	0.2704	0.2734	0.2764	0.2794	0.2823	0.2852
0.8	0.2881	0.2910	0.2939	0.2967	0.2995	0.3023	0.3051	0.3078	0.3106	0.3133
0.9	0.3159	0.3186	0.3212	0.3238	0.3264	0.3289	0.3315	0.3340	0.3365	0.3389
1.0	0.3413	0.3438	0.3461	0.3485	0.3508	0.3531	0.3554	0.3577	0.3599	0.3621
1.1	0.3643	0.3665	0.3686	0.3708	0.3729	0.3749	0.3770	0.3790	0.3810	0.3830
1.2	0.3849	0.3869	0.3888	0.3907	0.3925	0.3944	0.3962	0.3980	0.3997	0.4015
1.3	0.4032	0.4049	0.4066	0.4082	0.4099	0.4115	0.4131	0.4147	0.4162	0.4177
1.4	0.4192	0.4207	0.4222	0.4236	0.4251	0.4265	0.4279	0.4292	0.4306	0.4319
1.5	0.4332	0.4345	0.4357	0.4370	0.4382	0.4394	0.4406	0.4418	0.4429	0.4441
1.6	0.4452	0.4463	0.4474	0.4484	0.4495	0.4505	0.4515	0.4525	0.4535	0.4545
1.7	0.4554	0.4564	0.4573	0.4582	0.4591	0.4599	0.4608	0.4616	0.4625	0.4633
1.8	0.4641	0.4649	0.4656	0.4664	0.4671	0.4678	0.4686	0.4693	0.4699	0.4706
1.9	0.4713	0.4719	0.4726	0.4732	0.4738	0.4744	0.4750	0.4756	0.4761	0.4767
2.0	0.4772	0.4778	0.4783	0.4788	0.4793	0.4798	0.4803	0.4808	0.4812	0.4817
2.1	0.4821	0.4826	0.4830	0.4834	0.4838	0.4842	0.4846	0.4850	0.4854	0.4857
2.2	0.4861	0.4864	0.4868	0.4871	0.4875	0.4878	0.4881	0.4884	0.4887	0.4890
2.3	0.4893	0.4896	0.4898	0.4901	0.4904	0.4906	0.4909	0.4911	0.4913	0.4916
2.4	0.4918	0.4920	0.4922	0.4925	0.4927	0.4929	0.4931	0.4932	0.4934	0.4936
2.5	0.4938	0.4940	0.4941	0.4943	0.4945	0.4946	0.4948	0.4949	0.4951	0.4952
2.6	0.4953	0.4955	0.4956	0.4957	0.4959	0.4960	0.4961	0.4962	0.4963	0.4964
2.7	0.4965	0.4966	0.4967	0.4968	0.4969	0.4970	0.4971	0.4972	0.4973	0.4974
2.8	0.4974	0.4975	0.4976	0.4977	0.4977	0.4978	0.4979	0.4979	0.4980	0.4981
2.9	0.4981	0.4982	0.4982	0.4983	0.4984	0.4984	0.4985	0.4985	0.4986	0.4986
3.0	0.4987	0.4987	0.4987	0.4988	0.4988	0.4989	0.4989	0.4989	0.4990	0.4990

Chapter

1

Accounting for management

Chapter learning objectives

Upon completion of this chapter you will be able to:

- distinguish between data and information
- identify and explain the attributes of good information
- outline the managerial processes of planning, decision making and control
- explain the difference between strategic, tactical and operational planning
- distinguish between cost, profit, investment and revenue centres
- describe the differing needs for information of cost, profit, investment and revenue centres managers
- describe the purpose and role of cost and management accounting within an organisation
- compare and contrast financial accounting with cost and management accounting
- explain the limitations of management information in providing guidance for managerial decision-making

One of the PER performance objectives (PO1) is to take into account all relevant information and use professional judgement, your personal values and scepticism to evaluate data and make decisions. You should identify right from wrong and escalate anything of concern. You also need to make sure that your skills, knowledge and behaviour are up-to-date and allow you to be effective in you role. Working through this chapter should help you understand how to demonstrate that objective.

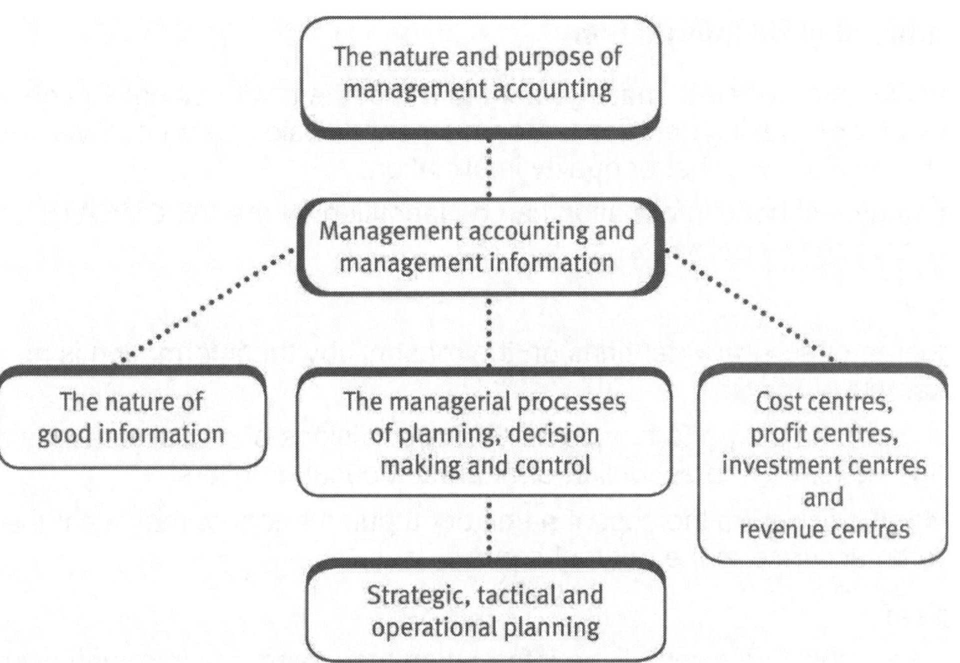

1 The nature of good information

Data and information

'Data' means facts. Data consists of numbers, letters, symbols, raw facts, events and transactions which have been recorded but not yet processed into a form suitable for use.

Information is data which has been processed in such a way that it is meaningful to the person who receives it (for making decisions).

- The terms data and information are often used interchangeably in everyday language.
- As data is converted into information, some of the detail of the data is eliminated and replaced by summaries which are easier to understand.

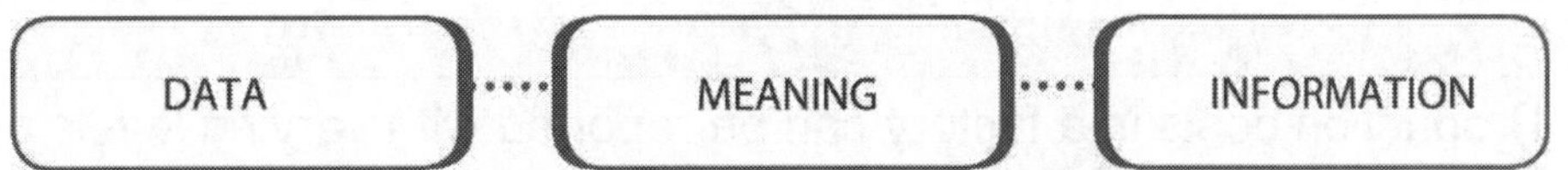

Test your understanding 1

What, if any, is the difference between data and information?

A They are the same

B Data can only be figures, whereas information can be facts or figures

C Information results from sorting and analysing data

D Data results from obtaining many individual pieces of information.

Attributes of good information

Information is provided to management to assist them with planning, controlling operations and making decisions. Management decisions are improved when they are provided with better quality information.

The attributes of good information can be identified by the **'ACCURATE'** acronym as shown below:

Accurate

The degree of accuracy depends on the reason why the information is needed. For example:

- a report on the performance of different divisions of a business may show figures to the nearest dollar, or nearest thousand dollars.
- when calculating the cost of a unit of output, managers may want the cost to be accurate to the nearest cent.

Complete

Managers should be given all the information they need, but information should not be excessive. For example:

- a complete control report on variances should include all standard and actual costs necessary to aid understanding of the variance calculations.
- production managers will need the variance analysis relating to material usage where-as purchasing managers with need the variance analysis relating to material prices.

Cost-effective

The value of information should exceed the cost of producing it. Management information is valuable, because it assists decision making. If a decision backed by information is different from what it would have been without the information, the value of information equates to the amount of money saved as a result.

Illustration 1 – Marginal cost versus marginal benefit

Production costs in a factory can be reported with varying levels of frequency ranging from daily (365 times per year) to annually (once per year). Costs and benefits of reporting relate to the frequency of reporting.

- Information has to be gathered, collated and reported in proportion to frequency and costs will move in line with this.
- Initially, benefits increase sharply, but this increase starts to tail off. A point may come where 'information overload' sets in and benefits actually start to decline and even become negative. If managers are overwhelmed with information this can actually get in the way of completing a job.

This can be shown graphically:

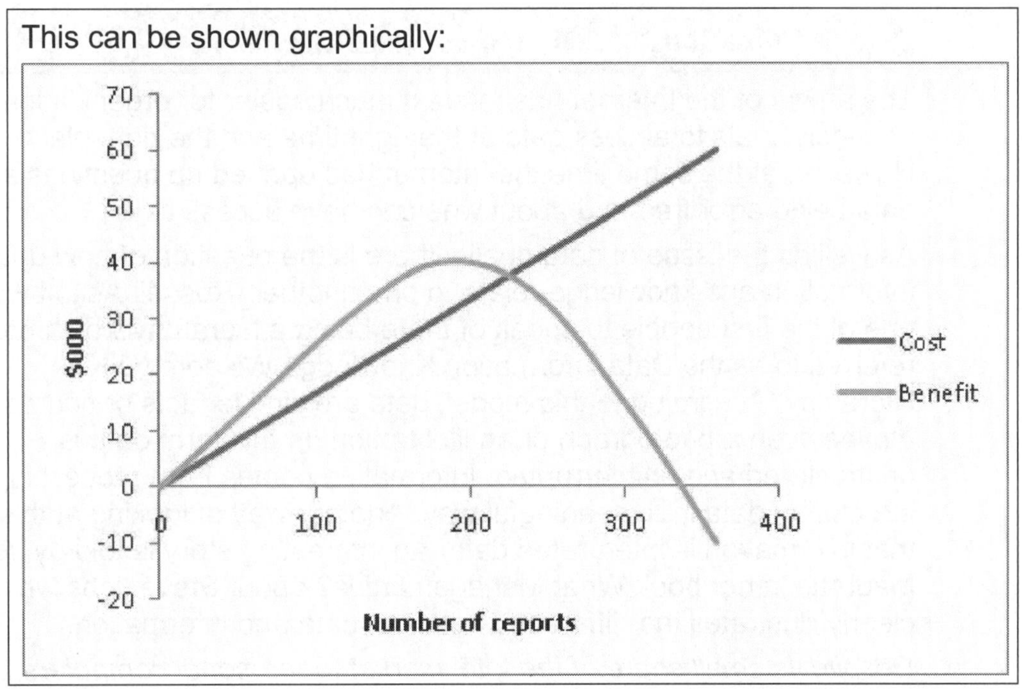

Understandable

Use of technical language or jargon must be limited. Accountants must always be careful about the way in which they present financial information to non-financial managers.

Relevant

The information contained within a report should be relevant to its purpose. Redundant parts should be removed. For example:

- the sales team may need to know the total cost of producing a unit to calculate the selling price but will not need to know the breakdown into material, labour and overhead costs.

Authoritative

Information should be trusted and provided from reliable sources so that the users can have confidence in their decision making

Timely

Information should be provided to a manager in time for decisions to be made based on that information.

Easy to use

We must always think about the person using the information we provide and make sure the information meets their needs

Data, Information, Knowledge and Wisdom

The arrival of the Internet has made it much easier for organisations and individuals to access data at the right time and the right place. However, at the same time the Internet has opened up questions about data being error free and about who can have access to it.

As well as the issue of data quality there is the question of how data, information and knowledge relate to one another. Russell Ackoff was one of the first people to speak of there being a hierarchy which he referred to as the Data Information Knowledge Wisdom (DIKW) Hierarchy. According to this model, data are simple facts or figures or maybe even a photograph or an illustration. In this form data is unstructured and uninterrupted. Information comes from processing or structuring data in a meaningful way. Another way of looking at this is that information is interpreted data. An interesting story is told by Joan Magretta in her book What Management is? about Steve Jobs which clearly illustrates the difference between data and information.

Despite its small share of the total market for personal computers, Apple has long been a leader in sales to schools and universities. When CEO Steve Jobs learned that Apple's share of computer sales to schools was 12.5 per cent in 1999, he was dismayed, but unless you're an industry analyst who knows the numbers cold, you won't appreciate just how dismayed he was. That's because, in 1998, Apple was the segment leader with a market share of 14.6 per cent. And, while Apple slipped to the number two spot in 1999, Dell grew and took the lead with 15.1 per cent. Alone each number is meaningless. Together they spell trouble, if you're Steve Jobs, you see a trend that you'd better figure out how to reverse. This isn't number crunching, its sense making. (Magretta, 2003, p. 123)

In this example the 12.5 per cent was data and when it was seen in conjunction with the 15.1 per cent it became information.

Knowledge is again different to data and information. Knowledge is much more personal and the presence or absence of knowledge can normally only be seen through the actions of individuals. When knowledge is written down it effectively becomes information.

Finally with respect to wisdom it is difficult to define this concept. Wisdom has something to do with understanding or insight. It is to do with achieving a good long-term outcome in relation to the circumstances you are in.

2 Mission statements

Before any planning can take place the **mission** of the business needs to be established.

The mission statement is a statement in writing that describes the overall aims of an organisation, that is, what it is trying to accomplish. In other words, it sets out the whole purpose of the business.

There are four key elements to a mission statement:

- **Purpose** – why does the business exist and who does it exist for?
- **Strategy** – what does the business provide and how is it provided?
- **Policies and culture** – how does the business expect its staff to act/behave?
- **Values** – What are the core principles of the business?

The mission should express what the business wants to achieve overall and the aims and objectives managers produce should all work towards achieving this.

Mission statements will have some or all of the following characteristics:

- Usually a brief statement of no more than a page in length
- Very general statement of entity culture
- States the aims of the organisation
- States the business areas in which the organisation intends to operate
- Open-ended (not in quantifiable terms)
- Does not include commercial terms, such as profit
- Not time-assigned
- Forms a basis of communication to the people inside the organisation and to people outside the organisation
- Used to formulate goal statements, objectives and short term targets
- Guides the direction of the entity's strategy and as such is part of management information.

Kaplan UK's mission statement is:

Kaplan helps individuals achieve their educational and career goals. We build futures one success story at a time.

Our core values define our company culture and provide the framework for what we deliver to our customers and employees each day.

- **Integrity** – We hold ourselves to the highest ethical standards in everything we do.
- **Knowledge** – We offer expert resources to help you achieve your academic and career best.
- **Support** – We give you the tools you need to succeed.
- **Opportunity** – We open doors and broaden access to education.
- **Results** – We're dedicated to helping you achieve your goals – we succeed when you succeed.

Examples of mission statements

Honda

Maintaining a global viewpoint, we are dedicated to supplying products of the highest quality, yet at a reasonable price for worldwide customer satisfaction.

The Walt Disney Company

The mission of The Walt Disney Company is to be one of the world's leading producers and providers of entertainment and information. Using our portfolio of brands to differentiate our content, services and consumer products, we seek to develop the most creative, innovative and profitable entertainment experiences and related products in the world.

Virgin Atlantic

Safety, security and consistent delivery of the basics are the foundation of everything we do.

The success of our three year strategy requires us to build on these foundations by focusing on the business and leisure markets and driving efficiency and effectiveness.

Tesco PLC

Our vision is for Tesco to be most highly valued by the customers we serve, the communities in which we operate, our loyal and committed staff and our shareholders; to be a growth company; a modern and innovative company and winning locally, applying our skills globally.

Battersea Dogs' & Cats' Home

We aim to never turn away a dog or cat in need of help, caring for them until their owners or loving new homes can be found, no matter how long it takes. We are champions for, and supporters of, vulnerable dogs and cats, determined to create lasting changes for animals in our society. Every year, we care for over 7,000 dogs and cats.

3 The managerial processes of planning, decision making and control

The main functions that management are involved with are planning, decision making and control.

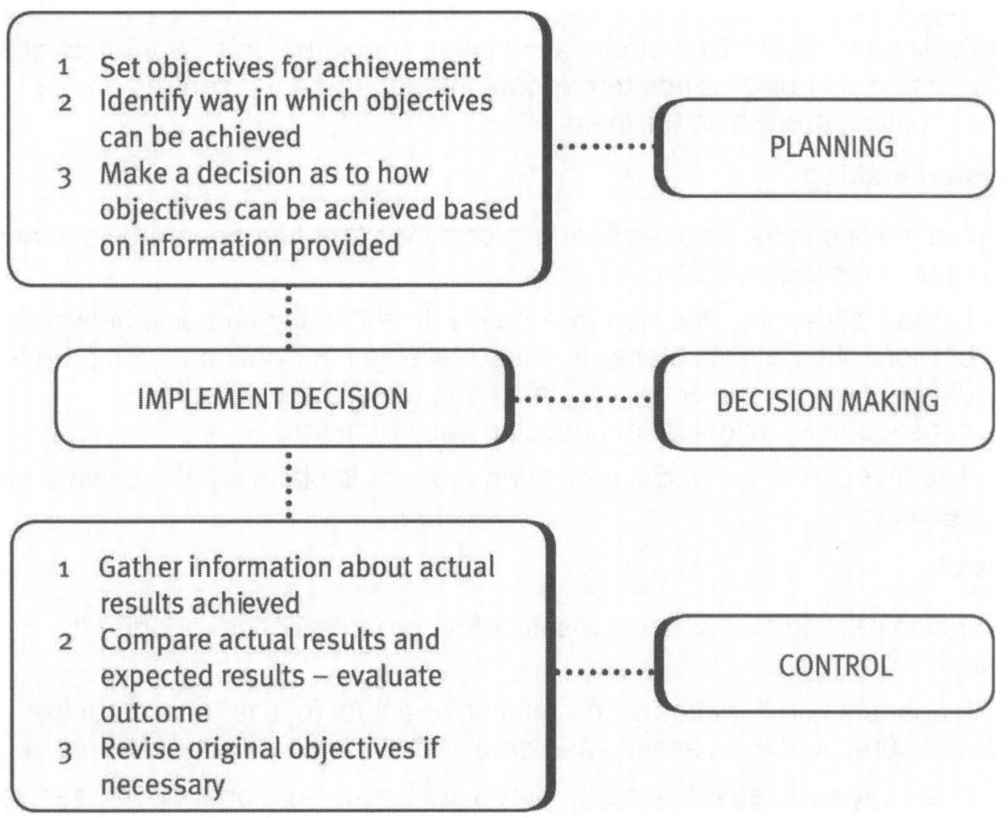

Planning

- Planning involves establishing the objectives of an organisation and formulating relevant strategies that can be used to achieve those objectives. In order to make plans, it helps to know what has happened in the past so that decisions about what is achievable in the future can be made. For example, if a manager is planning future sales volumes, he needs to know what the sales volumes have been in the past.
- Planning can be either short-term (tactical planning) or long-term (strategic planning).
- Planning is looked at in more detail in the next section of this chapter.

During the planning process the mission statement of a business is used to produce effective aims and objectives for employees and the company as a whole. Aims and objectives should be **SMART:**

- **Specific** – are the objectives well defined and understandable?
- **Measurable** – can achievement of the objectives be measured so that completion can be confirmed?
- **Attainable/Achievable** – can the objectives set be achieved with the resources and skills available?

- **Relevant** – are the objectives relevant for the people involved and to the mission of the business?
- **Timed** – are deadlines being set for the objectives that are achievable? Are there any stage reviews planned to monitor progress towards the objective?

By following the SMART hierarchy a business should be able to produce plans that lead to **goal congruence** throughout the departments, centres and/or regional offices (the whole business).

Decision making

Decision making involves considering information that has been provided and making an informed decision.

- In most situations, decision making involves making a choice between two or more alternatives. Managers need reliable information to compare the different courses of action available and understand what the consequences might be of choosing each of them.
- The first part of the decision-making process is planning, the second part is control.

Control

Information relating to the actual results of an organisation is reported to managers.

- Managers use the information relating to actual results to take control measures and to re-assess and amend their original budgets or plans.
- Internally-sourced information, produced largely for control purposes, is called feedback.
- The 'feedback loop' is demonstrated in the following illustration.

Illustration 2 – The managerial processes of planning, decision

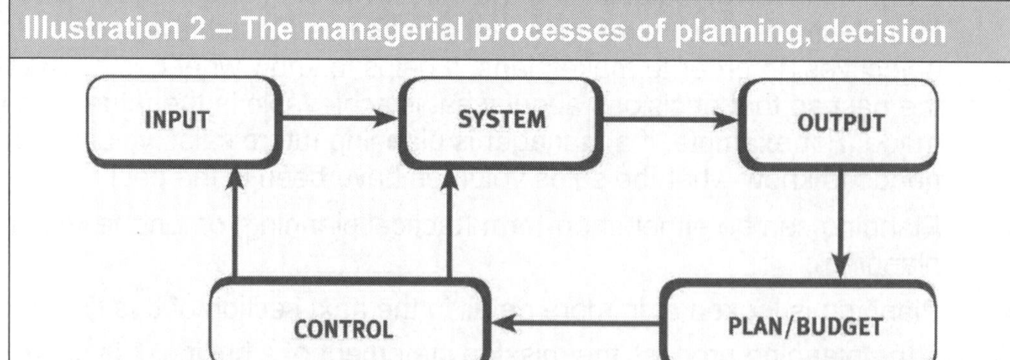

Here, management prepare a plan, which is put into action by the managers with control over the input resources (labour, money, materials, equipment and so on). Output from operations is measured and reported ('fed back') to management, and actual results are compared against the plan in control reports. Managers take corrective action where appropriate, especially in the case of exceptionally bad or good performance. Feedback can also be used to revise plans or prepare the plan for the next period.

Test your understanding 2

Required:

Complete the table identifying each function as planning, decision making and/or control.

	Planning	Control	Decision making
Preparation of the annual budget for a cost centre			
Revise budgets for next period for a cost centre			
Implement decisions based on information provided			
Set organisation's objectives for next period			
Compare actual and expected results for a period			

4 Levels of planning

There are three different levels of planning (known as 'planning horizons'). These three levels differ according to their time span and the seniority of the manager responsible for the tasks involved.

Strategic planning

'Strategic planning' can also be known as 'long-term planning' or 'corporate planning'. It considers:

- the longer term (five years plus)
- the whole organisation.

Senior managers formulate long-term objectives (goals) and plans (strategies) for an organisation as a whole. These objectives and plans should all be aiming to achieving the company's mission.

Tactical planning

Tactical planning takes the strategic plan and breaks it down into manageable chunks i.e. shorter term plans for individual areas of the business to enable the strategic plan to be achieved.

Senior and middle managers make short to medium term plans for the next year.

Operational planning

Operational planning involves making day-to-day decisions about what to do next and how to deal with problems as they arise.

All managers are involved in day to day decisions.

A simple hierarchy of management tasks can be presented as follows:

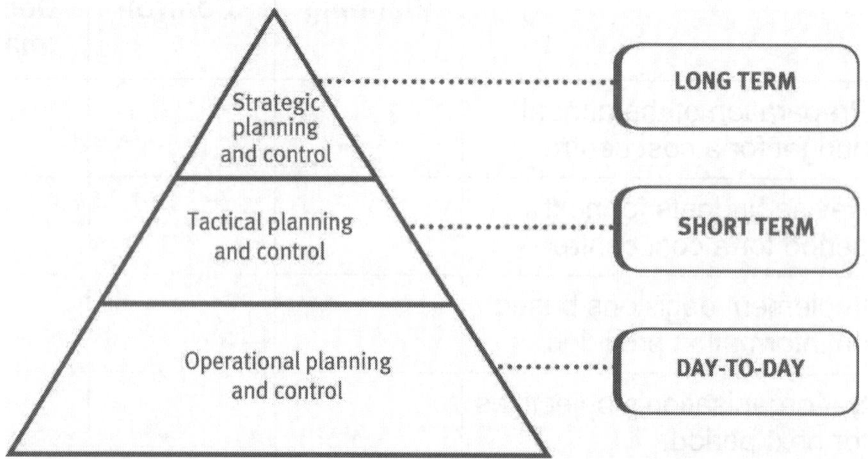

Strategic, tactical and operational planning

The table shown below illustrates the three different categories of planning.

	Private school	Profit-seeking business
Objective (mission)	To provide a high quality of education so that, within five years, 95% of pupils achieve grades A or B in their final examinations.	To achieve a 20% return on capital every year. To increase earnings per share by 10% every year for the next five years.
Strategic plans	Reduce class sizes. Raise new funds to invest $1 million in new equipment and facilities. Attract the highest quality of teacher by paying good salaries.	Cut costs by 15% in domestic markets. Expand into markets in Asia. Increase domestic market share by 10% in the next five years.

Tactical plans	Set a target for this year for examination results. Increase the number of teachers by 10% by the end of the year. Plan the launch of a fund- raising campaign	Carry out a cost reduction program next year. Establish business relationships with customers in Asia and carry out market research. Increase the size of the work force in order to improve total sales.
Operational plans	Prepare teaching schedules for the next term. Monitor the marks gained by students in mock examinations. Provide whiteboard training to teaching staff.	Obtain prices from more than one supplier before purchasing materials. Offer a bulk purchase discount of 10% to a major customer.

Test your understanding 3

The Management Accountant has communicated a detailed budget to ensure that cost savings targets are achieved in the forthcoming period.

This is an example of:

A Operational planning

B Tactical planning

C Strategic planning

D Business planning

5 Cost, revenue, profit and investment centres

Responsibility accounting

Responsibility accounting is based on identifying individual parts of a business which are the responsibility of a single manager.

A **responsibility centre** is an individual part of a business whose manager has personal responsibility for its performance.

Cost centres

A **cost centre** is a production or service location, function, activity or item of equipment whose costs are identified and recorded.

- For a paint manufacturer cost centres might be: mixing department; packaging department; administration; or marketing departments.
- For an accountancy firm, the cost centres might be: audit; taxation; accountancy; administration; canteen. Alternatively, they might be the various geographical locations, e.g. the London office, the Rome office, the Peru office.
- Cost centre managers need to have information about costs that are incurred and charged to their cost centres.
- The performance of a cost centre manager is judged on the extent to which cost targets have been achieved.

Revenue centres

A **revenue centre** is a part of the organisation that earns sales revenue. It is similar to a cost centre, but only revenues, and not costs, are recorded.

- Revenue centres are generally associated with selling activities, for example, regional sales managers may have responsibility for the regional sales revenues generated.
- Each regional manager would probably have sales targets to reach and would be held responsible for reaching these targets.
- Sales revenues earned must be able to be traced back to individual (regional) revenue centres so that the performance of individual revenue centre managers can be assessed.

Profit centres

A **profit centre** is a part of the business for which both the costs incurred and the revenues earned are identified.

- Profit centres are often found in large organisations with a divisionalised structure, and each division is treated as a profit centre.
- Within each profit centre, there could be several costs centres and revenue centres.
- The performance of a profit centre manager is measured in terms of the profit made by the centre.
- The manager must therefore be responsible for both costs and revenues and in a position to plan and control both.
- Data and information relating to both costs and revenues must be collected and allocated to the relevant profit centres.

Investment centres

Managers of investment centres are responsible for investment decisions as well as decisions affecting costs and revenues.

- Investment centre managers are therefore accountable for the performance of capital employed as well as profits (costs and revenues).
- The performance of investment centres is measured in terms of the profit earned relative to the capital invested (employed). This is known as the return on capital employed (ROCE).
- An example of an investment centres could be the UK and European divisions of a multinational company

6 Financial, cost and management accounting

Financial accounting

Financial accounting involves recording the financial transactions of an organisation and summarising them in periodic financial statements for external users who wish to analyse and interpret the financial position of the organisation.

- The main duties of the financial accountant include: maintaining the bookkeeping system of the nominal ledger, payables control account, receivables control account and so on and to prepare financial statements as required by law and accounting standards.
- Information produced by the financial accounting system is usually insufficient for the needs of management for decision making.

Cost and Management accounting

Managers usually want to know about the costs and the profits of individual products and services. In order to obtain this information, details are needed for each cost, revenue, profit and investment centre. Such information is provided by cost accounting and management accounting systems.

Cost accounting is a system for recording data and producing information about costs for the products produced by an organisation and/or the services it provides. It is also used to establish costs for particular activities or responsibility centres.

- Cost accounting involves a careful evaluation of the resources used within the enterprise.
- The techniques employed in cost accounting are designed to provide financial information about the performance of the enterprise and possibly the direction that future operations should take.
- The terms 'cost accounting' and 'management accounting' are often used to mean the same thing.
- Management accounting has cost accounting at its essential foundation.

Non-financial information

Information provided by cost accounting systems is financial in nature. Financial information is important for management because many objectives of an organisation are financial in nature, such as making profits and avoiding insolvency. Managers also need information of a non-financial nature.

- At a strategic level, management need to know about developments in their markets and in the economic situation. They also need to know about any new technology that emerges, and about the activities of competitors.
- At a tactical level, they might want to know about issues such as product or service quality, speed of handling customer complaints, customer satisfaction levels, employee skills levels and employee morale.
- At an operational level, they may want to know about the number of rejects per machine, the lead time for delivering materials and the number of labour and machine hours available.

The management accounting systems in many organisations are able to obtain non-financial as well as financial information for reporting to management. The importance of non-financial information within the reporting system should not be forgotten.

Differences between management accounting and financial accounting

The following illustration compares management accounting with financial accounting.

Illustration 3 – Management versus financial accounting

	Management accounting	Financial accounting
Information mainly produced for	Internal use e.g. managers and employees.	External use e.g. shareholders, payables, lenders, banks, government.
Purpose of information	To aid planning, controlling and decision making.	To record the financial performance in a period and the financial position at the end of that period.
Legal requirements	None.	Limited companies must produce financial accounts.
Formats	Management decide on the information they require and the most useful way of presenting it.	Format and content of financial accounts intending to give a true and fair view should follow accounting standards and company law.
Nature of information	Financial and non-financial.	Mostly financial.
Time period	Historical and forward-looking.	Mainly a historical record.

The role of management accounting within an organisation's management information system

The management information system of an organisation is likely to be able to prepare the following:

- annual statutory accounts
- budgets and forecasts
- product profitability reports
- cash flow reports
- capital investment appraisal reports
- standard cost and variance analysis reports
- returns to government departments, e.g. Sales Tax returns.

Management information is generally supplied to management in the form of reports. Reports may be routine reports prepared on a regular basis (e.g. monthly) or they may be prepared for a special purpose (e.g. ad hoc report).

Test your understanding 4

The following assertions relate to management accounting:

(i) The purpose of management accounting is to provide accounting information to the managers of the business and other internal users.

(ii) Management accounts are only concerned with the cost of goods, services and operations.

Which of the following statements are true?

A Assertion (i) and (ii) are both correct

B Only assertion (i) is correct

C Only assertion (ii) is correct

D Neither assertion (i) or (ii) is correct

7 The limitations of management information

There are a number of respects in which management accounting information may fail to meet its objective of assisting management in the decision making process.

These can be summarised as follows:

Failure to comply with the qualities of useful information

If information supplied to managers is deficient in any of these respects then inappropriate management decisions may be made. Consider the following:

- **Accuracy** – overestimating costs may result in a decision not to produce a product which in fact is profitable; on the other hand, overestimating the price at which the output can be sold may result in the organisation producing output which cannot be sold in sufficient volume to be profitable.
- **Timeliness** – in connection with a decision to close a division or department if the information is presented to management after a decision had been made to lay off staff that could have been profitably employed in other divisions or activities, the company has incurred unnecessary redundancy costs, lost possible future revenues and demotivated the remaining employees when they learn of the redundancies.
- **Understandable** – excessive focus by management accountants on more complex techniques of which general management have little or no knowledge or understanding may mean that the accountant's advice will be ignored. There is significant attention being given to the role of the management accountant as an educator within the organisation – explaining the information and training general management to help them to understand the information better.

Relevant costs and revenues

Not all information produced by an accounting system is relevant to the decisions made by management. In particular, information produced mainly for financial reporting purposes and then taken as the basis for management decisions will often need significant modification to be useful to management. The principle here is that the figures presented to assist in management decision-making are those that will be affected by the decision, i.e. they should be:

- **Future** – costs and revenues that are going to be incurred sometime in the future. Costs and revenues that have already been incurred are known as sunk costs and are not relevant to the decision to be made.
- **Incremental** – the **extra** cost or revenue that is created as a result of a decision taken.
- **Cash flows** – actual cash being spent or received not monetary items that are produced via accounting convention e.g. book or carrying values, depreciation charges.

Non-financial information

Managers will not always be guided by the sort of financial and other (hard) information supplied by the management accounting system. They will also look at qualitative, behavioural, motivational, even environmental factors. These non-financial factors can be just as important in relation to a decision as financial information – but they are often more difficult to estimate and quantify.

Illustration 4 – Non-financial factors

A processing company needs to increase its output in order to take advantage of an increase in the total market for its product.

Alternative A

To provide additional production capacity a new factory extension could be built. However, there is a danger that the extension will be seen by the local council and by residents as an eyesore. Some landscaping and re-design work may be carried out at extra cost to company to make the extension more environmentally acceptable.

Alternative B

This entails keeping the factory at its current size but increasing the working hours per week for all production staff by 20%. The latter may be a cheaper solution in financial terms but may have an adverse impact on staff morale and result in a significant increase in staff turnover.

It is not easy for the company to build the non-financial costs into its decision making process as they are often difficult to quantify.

External information

The environment refers to all of the external factors which affect a company and includes government actions, competitor actions, customer demands and other factors for example the weather.

Conventional accounting systems focus entirely on internal information such as production costs and volume of output produced. Companies and organisations do not, of course exist in a vacuum – they live in an environment in which they are influenced by a number of other organisations and forces arising from outside the organisation itself. This leads into an area of study often referred to as environmental analysis.

We do not need to go into this area in detail here, but, as with the non-financial factors referred to above, you should be aware that the environment (this is simply the external circumstances in which the company operates) will have an influence on a company's actions which should be reflected in its decision making processes.

It follows from this that an organisation should have information on its environment available to it within its accounting information systems – the organisation needs external information as well as internal information.

8 Chapter summary

The nature and purpose of management accounting

Management accounting and management information
- Financial accounting
- Cost accounting
- Management accounting

The nature of good information
Accurate
Complete
Cost-effective
Understandable
Relevant
Accessible
Timely
Easy to use

Cost centres
– costs identified

Profit centres
– cost and revenues indentified

Investment centres
– profit centre with responsibility for investment

Revenue centres
– accountable for revenues only

The managerial processes of planning, decision making and control

Plan – establish objectives of organisation and relevant strategies

Decision making – make informed decision using management information

Control – take control measures/feedback loop

Strategic, tactical and operational planning

Strategic – long term
Tactical – short term
Operational – day-to-day

Test your understanding answers

Test your understanding 1

C

The two terms are frequently used synonymously but strictly speaking they mean different things. Data is obtained from a survey and is turned into information by sorting and analysis. Both data and information can comprise either facts or figures.

Test your understanding 2

	Planning	Control	Decision making
Preparation of the annual budget for a cost centre	√		√
Revise budgets for next period for a cost centre		√	√
Implement decisions based on information provided			√
Set organisation's objectives for next period	√		√
Compare actual and expected results for a period		√	√

Note that all planning and control functions are part of the decision making process and are therefore identified as being both. The only exception is 'implement decisions based on information provided' which is not part of planning and control, but the one decision making task that there is.

Test your understanding 3

B

The management accountant is providing a new budget for the forthcoming period – i.e. a senior manager making a short term plan.

Test your understanding 4

B

Management accounting provides managers and internal users with information to make decisions. Management accounts are concerned with more than only the cost of goods, services and operations such as quality and use of resources.

Chapter

2

Cost classification

Chapter learning objectives

Upon completion of this chapter you will be able to:

- explain and illustrate production and non-production costs
- describe the different elements of non-production cost – administrative, selling, distribution and finance
- describe the different elements of production cost – materials, labour and overheads
- explain the importance of the distinction between production and non-production costs when valuing output and inventories
- explain and illustrate with examples classifications used in the analysis of the product/service costs including by function, direct and indirect, fixed and variable, stepped fixed and semi variable costs
- describe and illustrate, graphically, different types of cost behaviour
- use high/low analysis to separate the fixed and variable elements of total costs including situations involving semi variable and stepped fixed costs and changes in the variable cost per unit
- explain the advantages and disadvantages of using high low method to estimate the fixed and variable element of costing
- explain the structure of linear functions and equations
- explain and illustrate the concepts of cost objects, cost units and cost centres
- explain and illustrate the use of codes in categorising transaction.

One of the PER performance objectives (PO12) is to apply different management accounting techniques is different business contexts to effectively manage and use resources. Working through this chapter should help you understand how to demonstrate that objective.

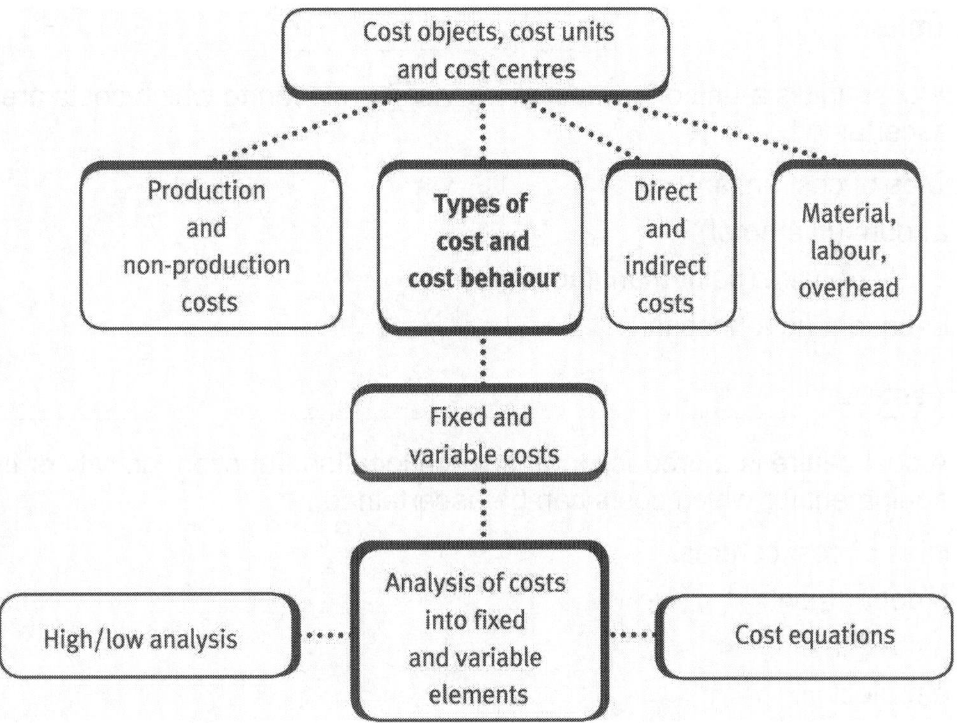

1 Analysing costs

Management will require a variety of different cost summaries, including:

- costs for a particular product – a cost unit or cost object
- costs for use in the preparation of external financial reports
- costs for a particular department – a cost centre
- costs to be used for decision making
- costs that are useful for planning and control.

To be able to produce these summaries the type of cost and the cost behaviour will need to be analysed.

Cost objects

A cost object is any activity for which a separate measurement of cost is undertaken.

Examples of cost objects:

- cost of a product
- cost of a service
- cost of running a department
- cost of running a regional office.

Cost units

A cost unit is a unit of product or service in relation to which costs are ascertained.

Examples of cost units:

- a room (in a hotel)
- a litre of paint (paint manufacturers)
- in-patient (in a hospital).

Cost centres

A cost centre is a production or service location, function, activity or item of equipment for which costs can be ascertained.

Examples of cost centres:

- a department
- a machine
- a project
- a ward (in a hospital).

Cost cards

A cost card is used to show the breakdown of the costs of producing output based on the classification of each cost. A cost card can be produced for one unit or a planned level of production.

The following costs are brought together and recorded on a cost card:

- direct materials
- direct labour
- direct expenses
- prime cost (total direct costs)
- variable production overheads
- fixed production overheads
- non-production overheads.

The terms used in the above bullet points are explained in the rest of the chapter.

Illustration 1 – Cost card

A cost card for a hand-made wooden train set is shown below.

- The cutting and assembly department and the painting department are cost centres.
- One hand-made wooden train set is a cost unit (but may also be classed as a cost object).

		\$ per unit
Direct materials:		
Wood	5m^2 @ \$2.50 per m^2	12.50
Paint	0.1 litres at \$10 per litre	1.00
Direct labour:		
Cutting and assembly department	0.5 hours at \$6.00 per hour	3.00
Painting department	1.0 hours @ \$7.00 per hour	7.00
Direct expenses:	Licence fee @ \$2 per train set	2.00
PRIME COST		25.50
Variable production overheads:		
Power for electric saws	0.25 hours @ \$2.00 per hour	0.50
TOTAL VARIABLE (MARGINAL) PRODUCTION COST		26.00
Fixed production overheads:		
	1.5 labour hours @ \$10.00 per labour hour	15.00
TOTAL PRODUCTION (ABSORPTION) COST		41.00
Non-production overheads:		
Administration, selling and distribution	20% of total production cost	8.20
TOTAL COST		49.20

Once the total cost is calculated then the selling price of a product can be calculated using either a mark-up or a margin. The mark-up or margin will be the profit made on each unit.

Mark-up (based on cost being 100%)

There is to be a 20% mark-up applied when calculating the selling price:

Mark-up = \$49.20/100 × 20 = \$9.84

Selling price = \$49.20 + \$9.84 = \$59.04

Margin (based on the selling price being 100%)

There is to be a margin of 10% applied when calculating the selling price:

Margin = \$49.20/90 × 10 = \$5.47

Selling price = \$49.20 + \$5.47 = \$54.67

2 Classifying costs

Costs can be classified in a number of different ways.

- **Element** – classify costs as to whether they relate to material, labour or expenses. This is useful for cost control.
- **Nature** – classify costs as to how they relate to production. Are they directly involved in the production of the product/service or indirectly involved in production? This is useful for cost accounting.
- **Function** – classify costs based on whether they are production costs or non-production costs. This is useful for the financial accounts.
- **Behaviour** – classify costs based on how they change in relation to levels of output or activity. This is useful for budgeting and decision making.

3 Classification by element

To classify by element you need to decide if a cost is a material cost, a labour cost or a cost relating to something else – an expense.

- **Materials** – all costs of materials purchased for production or non-production activities. For example, raw materials, components, cleaning materials, maintenance materials and stationery.
- **Labour** – all staff costs relating to employees on the payroll of the organisation.
- **Expenses** – all other costs which are not materials or labour. This includes all bought-in services, for example, rent, telephone, sub-contractors and costs such as the depreciation of equipment.

4 Classification by nature

Direct costs

Direct costs are costs which can be directly identified with a specific cost unit or cost centre.

There are three main types of direct cost – direct material, direct labour and direct expenses. The direct costs associated with a shirt (cost unit) manufactured by a clothing company would be:

- direct materials – cloth for making shirts
- direct labour – the wages of the workers stitching the cloth to make the shirts
- direct expenses – the royalties paid to a designer.

The total of direct costs is known as the **prime cost**.

Indirect costs

Indirect costs are costs which cannot be directly identified with a specific cost unit or cost centre.

The indirect costs associated with a shirt (cost unit) manufactured by a clothing company would be:

- indirect materials – these include materials that cannot be traced to an individual item for example cleaning fluids for cleaning the machinery
- indirect labour – the cost of a supervisor who supervises the shirt makers
- indirect expenses – the cost of renting the factory where the shirts are manufactured.

The total of indirect costs is known as **overheads**.

Direct and indirect cost?

It is important to realise that a particular cost may sometimes be a direct cost and sometimes an indirect cost. It depends on the cost object we are trying to cost.

For example, the salary of the machining department supervisor is a direct cost of that department or cost centre because it can be specifically identified with the department. However, it is an indirect cost of each of the cost units processed in the machining department because it cannot be specifically identified with any particular cost unit.

Test your understanding 1

Identify whether the following costs are materials, labour or expenses and whether they are direct or indirect for the production of toy cars.

Cost	Materials, labour or expense	Direct or indirect?
The hire of specific tools or equipment		
Rent of the factory		
Supervisors' salaries		
Oil for lubricating machines		
Wages of factory workers involved in production		
Depreciation of equipment		

Test your understanding 2

(a) Which of the following would be classed as indirect labour?

A Assembly workers

B A stores assistant in a factory storeroom

C Plasterers in a building company

D An audit clerk in an accountancy firm

(b) Direct costs are:

A costs which can be identified with a cost centre but not a single cost unit

B costs which can be identified with a single cost unit or cost centre

C costs which can be attributed to an accounting period

D none of the above

5 Classification by function

Production costs

Production costs are costs that relate to the manufacture of a product or provision of a service. These costs are found in the cost of sales section of the statement of profit or loss.

Production costs, such as direct materials, direct labour, direct expenses and production overheads, **are** included in the **valuation of inventory**.

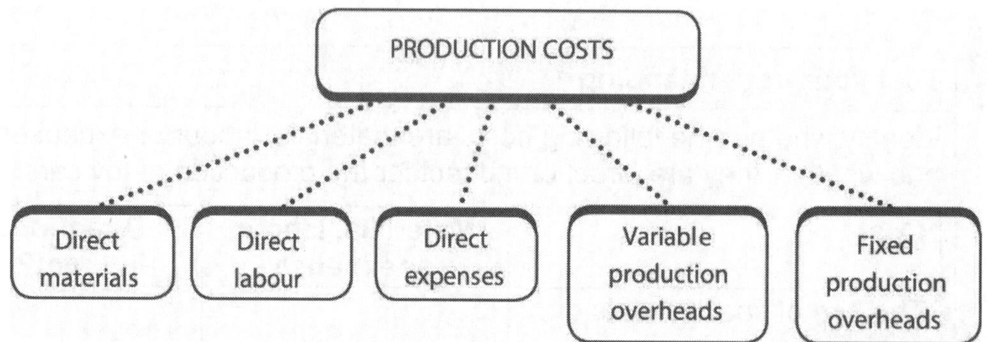

Examples of production costs

Examples of production costs for a construction company

- Direct materials – bricks, cement
- Direct labour – builders, plasterers, electricians
- Direct expenses – the cost of a subcontracted crane and driver
- Variable production overheads – electricity
- Fixed production overheads – site managers salary.

Non-production costs

Non-production costs are costs that are not directly associated with the production of the businesses output.

Non-production costs, such as administrative costs, selling costs and finance costs, are charged to the statement of profit or loss as expenses for the period in which they are incurred. Non-production costs **are not** included in the **valuation of inventory**.

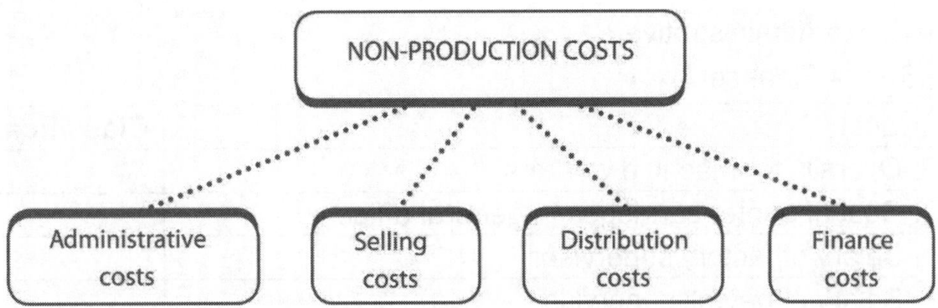

Examples of non-production costs

- Administrative costs – the costs involved in running the general administration departments of an organisation, for example, the accounts department.
- Selling costs – costs associated with taking orders from customers who wish to buy an organisation's products (sales department costs) and also marketing costs.
- Distribution costs – the costs involved in distributing an organisation's finished products, such as the cost of running the warehouse or delivery costs.
- Finance costs – the costs that are incurred in order to finance an organisation, for example, loan interest.

Test your understanding 3

Complete the following table by classifying each expense correctly.

Classifications

1 = Production

2 = Selling

3 = Distribution

4 = Administrative

5 = Finance

Cost	**Classification**
Overalls for machine workers	
Cost of printer cartridges in general office	
Salary of factory supervisor	
Salary of payroll supervisor	
Rent of warehouse for storing goods ready for sale	
Loan interest	
Salary of factory security guard	
Early settlement discounts for customers who pay early	
Salary of the Chairman's PA	
Road tax licence for delivery vehicles	
Bank overdraft fee	
Salesmen's commissions	

6 Classification by behaviour

Costs may be classified according to the way that they behave in relation to changes in levels of activity. Cost behaviour classifies costs as one of the following:

- variable cost
- fixed cost
- stepped fixed cost
- semi-variable cost.

Variable costs

Variable costs are costs that vary in direct proportion with the level of activity. As activity levels increase then total variable costs will also increase.

Variable costs can be shown graphically as follows:

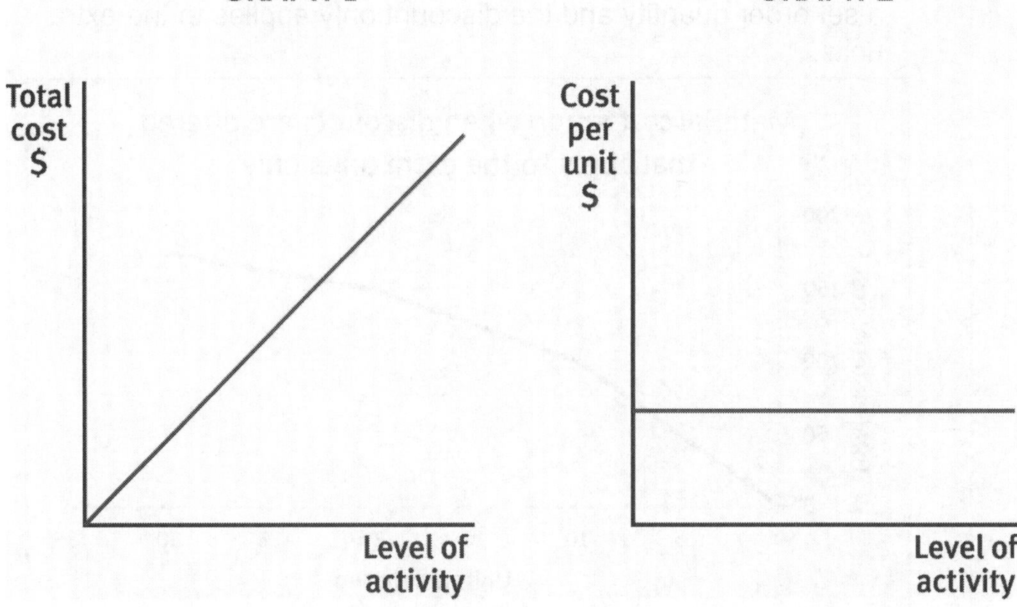

- Note that as total costs increase with activity levels, the cost per unit of variable costs remains constant.
- Examples of variable costs include direct costs such as raw materials and direct labour.

Numerical example of variable costs

- A factory is producing widgets. It takes $4m^2$ to make one widget and it costs $2 per square metre. If the factory makes 50 widgets it costs $400, if the factory makes 100 widgets it costs $800. The cost incurred increases in line with the volume being produced – graph 1 demonstrates this.
- The material for each widget costs 4 × $2 = $8 and it does not change if more or less widgets are made. The variable cost per unit remains constant – graph 2 demonstrates this.

Material cost and discounts

Direct material costs are assumed to have a variable cost behaviour but sometimes quantity discounts are available when purchases exceed a certain order size.

There are two main scenarios:

1 Discounts are received on additional purchases of material above a set order quantity and the discount only applies to the extra units.

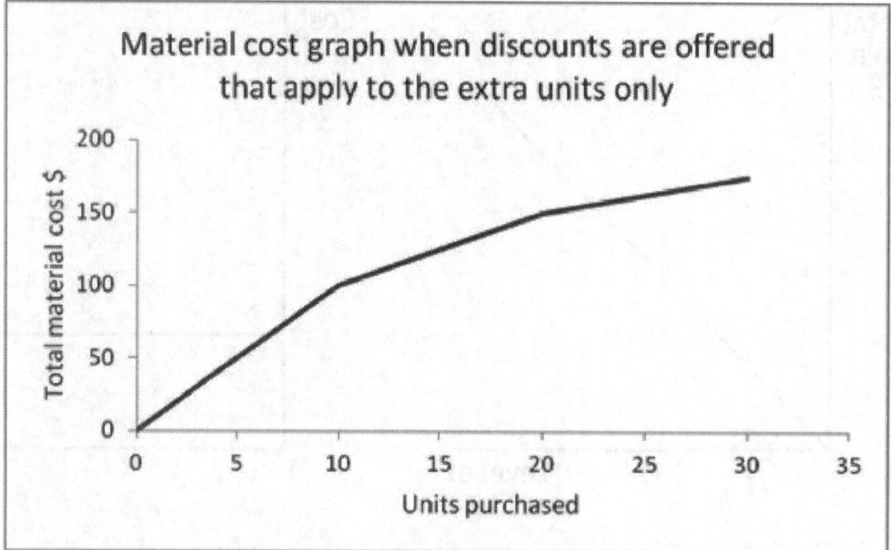

2 Discounts are received when total purchases exceed a certain level and all units purchased are invoiced at a lower cost per unit. Note: the data line will always return to the origin.

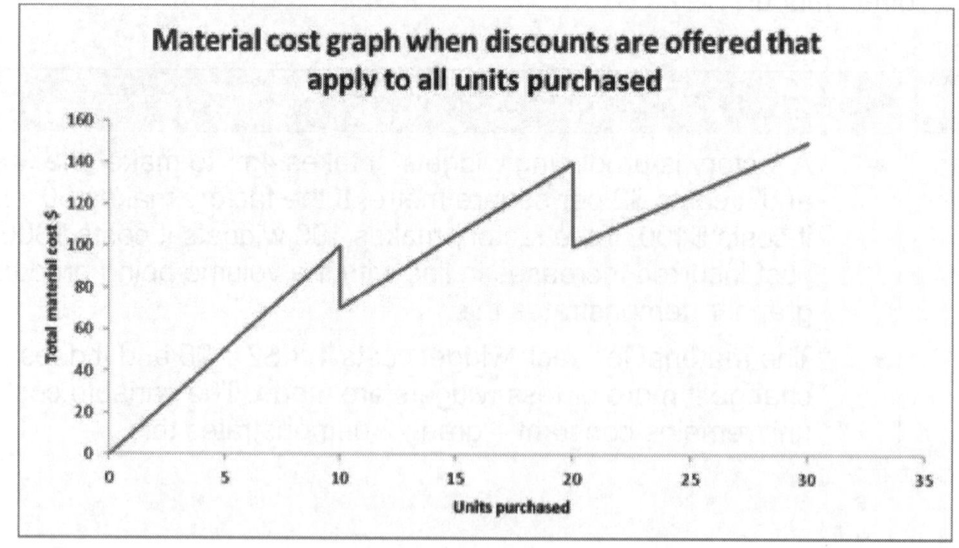

Fixed costs

A fixed cost is a cost which is incurred for an accounting period, and which, within certain activity levels remains constant.

Fixed costs can be shown graphically as follows:

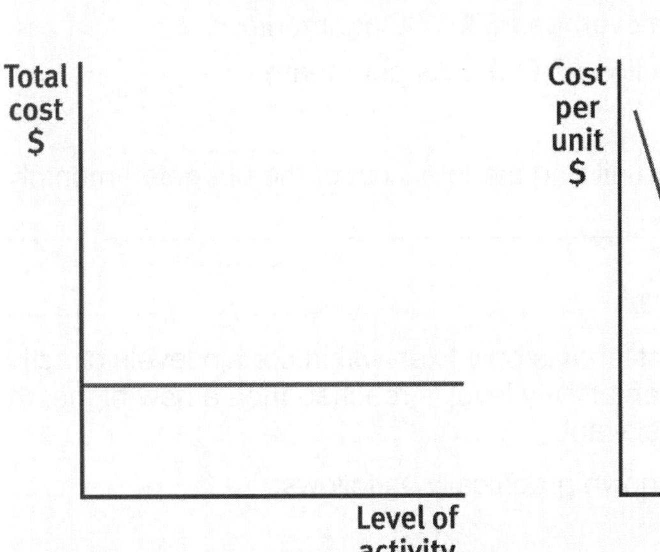

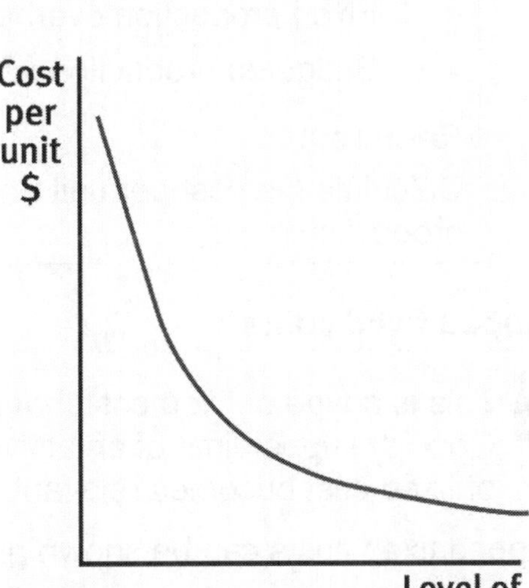

- Note that the total cost remains constant over a given level of activity but that the cost per unit falls as the level of activity increases.
- Examples of fixed costs:
  - rent
  - business rates
  - executive salaries.

Numerical example of fixed costs

- If factory rent is $5,000 per month, this cost will be incurred whether 2 widgets are made, or 200 widgets are made – graph 1 demonstrates this.
- If 2 widgets are made the fixed cost per unit is $5,000 ÷ 2, i.e. $2,500 per widget.
- If 200 widgets are made the fixed cost per unit is $5,000 ÷ 200, i.e. $25 per widget.
- Therefore, the fixed cost per unit falls at a reducing rate but never reaches zero – graph 2 demonstrates this.

Test your understanding 4

ILCB has the following information relating to one of its products:

- Direct material cost per unit $1
- Direct labour cost per unit $3
- Variable production cost per unit $3
- Fixed production overhead $30,000 per month
- Budgeted production 15,000 units per month

Required:

Calculate the cost per unit and the total cost of the budgeted monthly production?

Stepped fixed costs

This is a type of fixed cost that is only fixed within certain levels of activity. Once the upper limit of an activity level is reached then a new higher level of fixed cost becomes relevant.

Stepped fixed costs can be shown graphically as follows:

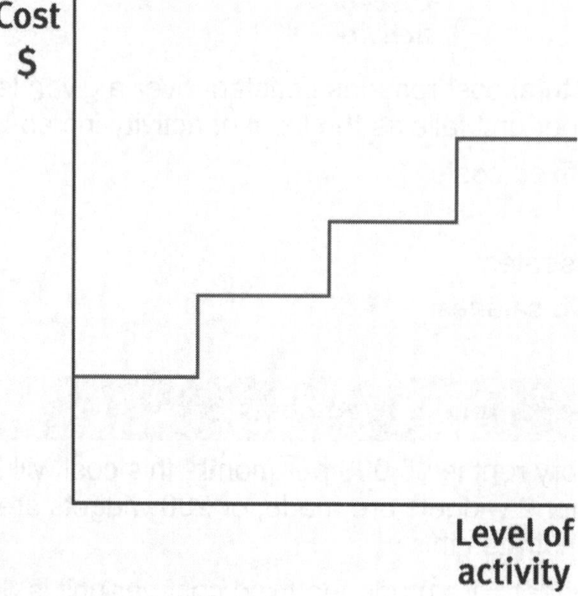

- Examples of stepped fixed costs:
  - warehousing costs (as more space is required, more warehouses must be purchased or rented)
  - supervisors' wages (as the number of employees increases, more supervisors are required).

Numerical example of stepped costs

- For production of up to 50 widgets, only one supervisor is required but if production is between 50 and 100 widgets, two supervisors are required.
- The cost of one supervisor is $18,000 per annum and the cost of two supervisors is therefore $36,000.
- The fixed costs therefore increase in steps.

Semi-variable costs

Semi-variable costs contain both fixed and variable cost elements and are therefore partly affected by changes in the level of activity.

Semi-variable costs can be shown graphically as follows:

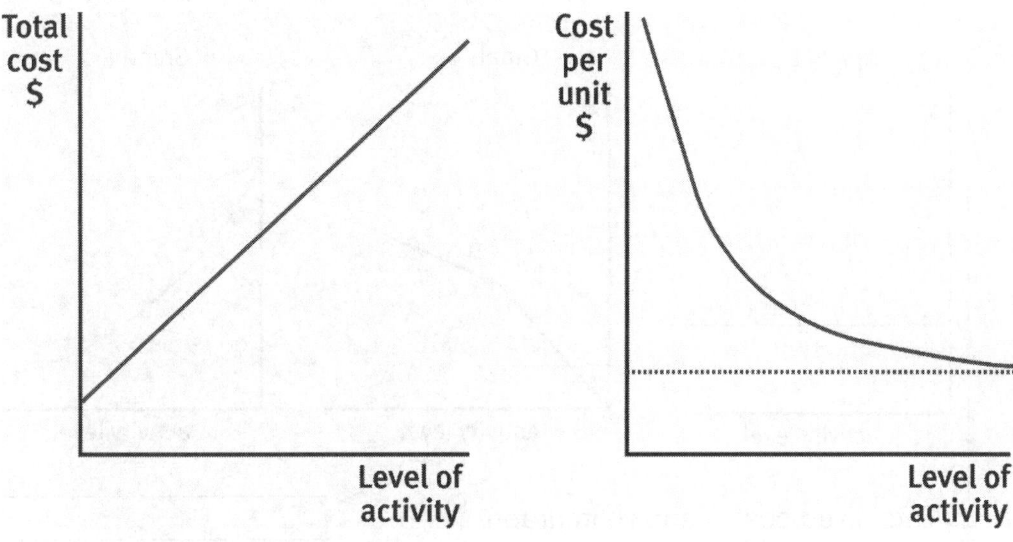

- Examples of semi-variable costs:
  - electricity bills (fixed standing charge plus variable cost per unit of electricity consumed)
  - telephone bills (fixed line rental plus variable cost per call).

Test your understanding 5

Classify the following items of expenditure according to their behaviour i.e. as fixed, variable, semi-variable or stepped fixed costs.

1	Monthly rent	5	Telephone bill
2	Council tax charge	6	Annual salary
3	Production line workers wages	7	Depreciation of 1, 2 or 3 machines
4	Electricity bill	8	Raw materials

Test your understanding 6

Study the following graphs, where the vertical axis represents 'Total Costs' or 'Cost per unit'. Then answer the questions shown below.

Graph 1

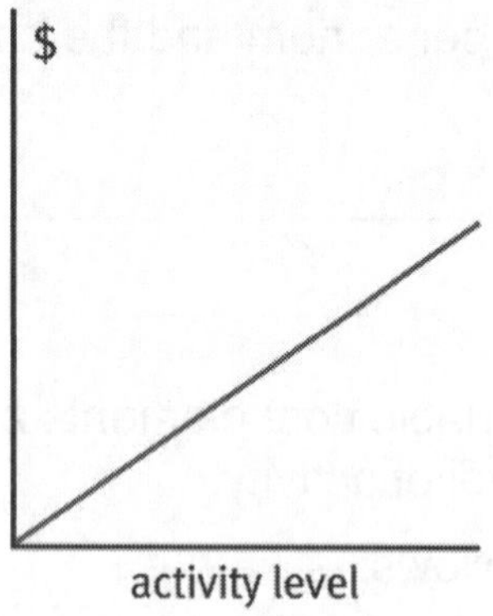

$

activity level

Graph 2

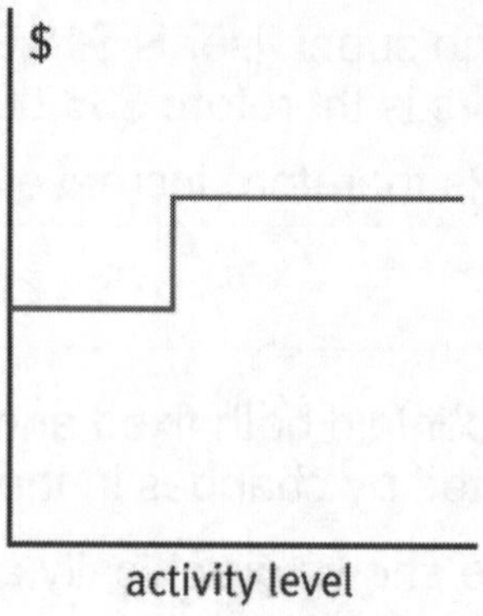

$

activity level

Graph 3

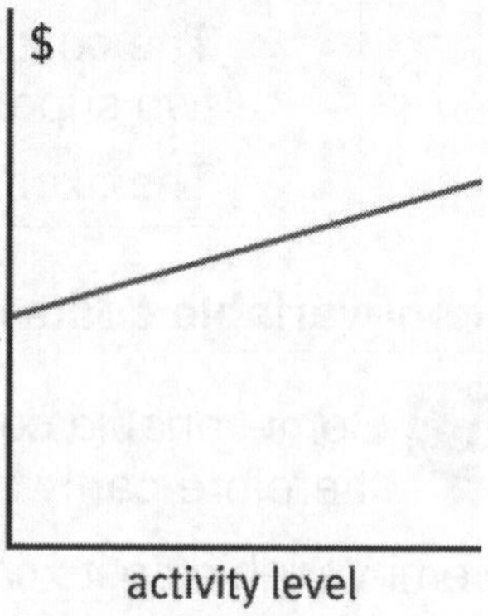

$

activity level

Graph 4

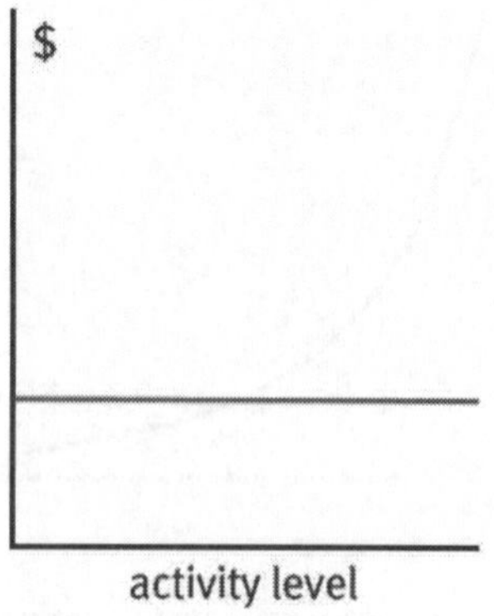

$

activity level

Graph 5

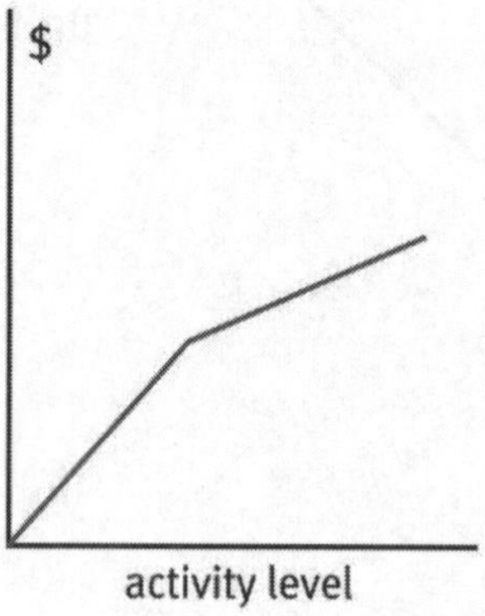

$

activity level

Graph 6

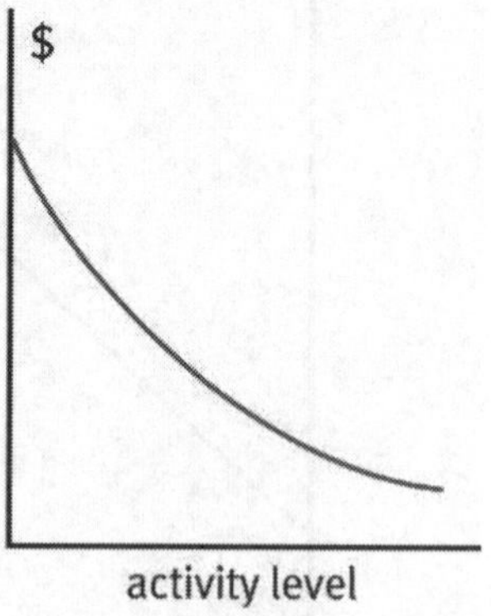

$

activity level

Total fixed cost is shown in graph	
Total variable cost is shown in graph	
Total semi-variable cost is shown in graph	
Fixed cost per unit is shown in graph	
Variable cost per unit is shown in graph	
A stepped fixed cost is shown in graph	

7 Identifying cost behaviours

The behavioural characteristics of costs are used when planning or forecasting costs at different levels of production or activity. When producing a forecast it may be necessary to identify the type of behaviour a cost is exhibiting. It is useful to remember the following:

- Fixed costs are constant in total
- Variable costs are constant per unit
- Semi-variable costs are neither constant in total nor constant per unit.
- Stepped fixed costs will be constant in total within a certain range.

Illustration 2 – Identifying cost behaviours

A company has a mix of variable, semi variable, fixed and stepped fixed costs.

Total cost at different activity levels

Cost	1,000 units	3,000 units	5,000 units	7,000 units
1	$19,000	$33,000	$47,000	$61,000
2	$1,920	$5,760	$9,600	$13,440
3	$7,000	$7,000	$7,000	$7,000
4	$12,500	$12,500	$17,000	$17,000

Cost per unit at different activity levels:

Cost	1,000 units	3,000 units	5,000 units	7,000 units
1	$19.00	$11.00	$9.40	$8.71
2	$1.92	$1.92	$1.92	$1.92
3	$7.00	$2.33	$1.40	$1.00
4	$12.50	$4.17	$3.40	$2.43

Identify the behaviour for each of the costs

- Cost 1 is a semi-variable cost as the total cost changes when activity level change and the cost per unit also changes at the different activity levels
- Cost 2 is a variable cost as the cost per unit is constant at each activity level
- Cost 3 is a fixed cost as the total cost does not change as activity level changes
- Cost 4 is a stepped fixed cost as the total cost is constant then increases to a new constant level and the cost per unit is changing at each activity level

8 The high/low method used for separating a semi-variable cost

The total cost of a semi-variable cost is:

Total costs = Total fixed costs + (Variable cost per unit × Activity level)

To be able to predict costs at different activity levels it is necessary to separate the fixed cost element from the variable cost element. The high-low method can be used to **approximate** the variable cost per unit and the total fixed cost.

The high/low method

Step 1

Select the highest and lowest **activity levels**, and their associated costs.

Step 2

Calculate the variable cost (VC) per unit:

$$\text{VC per unit} = \frac{\text{Cost at high level of activity} - \text{cost at low level of activity}}{\text{High level of activity} - \text{low level of activity}}$$

Step 3

Calculate the fixed cost by substitution, using either the high or low activity level.

Fixed cost = Total cost at activity level – (Variable cost × Activity level)

Step 4

Use the total fixed cost and the variable cost per unit values from steps 2 and 3 to calculate the estimated cost at different activity levels.

Total costs = Total fixed costs + (Variable cost per unit × Activity level)

Assumption underlying the high/low method

Assumptions of the high/low method are as follows:

- the only thing causing any change in cost is the change in activity
- the cost under consideration is potentially semi-variable (i.e. it has both fixed and variable elements)
- the linear model of cost behaviour is valid i.e. y = a + bx (we will study this in more detail later on in this chapter).

Illustration 3 – The high/low method

Output (units)	**Total cost** ($)
200	7,000
300	8,000
400	9,000

Required:

(a) Calculate the variable cost per unit.

(b) Calculate the total fixed cost.

(c) Estimate the total cost if output is 350 units.

(d) Estimate the total cost if output is 600 units.

Solution

(a) Variable cost per unit = ($9,000 – $7,000)/(400 – 200) = $2,000/200 = $10 per unit

(b) Total fixed cost by substituting at high activity level:

Total cost	=	$9,000
Total variable cost	= 400 × $10	$4,000
Therefore fixed cost	=	$5,000

(c) If output is 350units

Variable cost	= 350 × $10 =	$3,500
Fixed cost	=	$5,000
Total cost	=	$8,500

(d) If output is 600 units:

Variable cost	= 600 × $10 =	$6,000
Fixed cost	=	$5,000
Total cost	=	$11,000

Test your understanding 7

The total costs incurred at various output levels in a factory have been measured as follows:

Output (units)	**Total cost** ($)
26	6,566
30	6,510
33	6,800
44	6,985
48	7,380
50	7,310

Required:

Using the high/low method, analyse the total cost into fixed and variable components.

High/low method with stepped fixed costs

Sometimes fixed costs are only fixed within certain levels of activity (stepped fixed costs). The high/low method can still be used to estimate fixed and variable costs.

- Choose the two activity levels where the fixed costs remain unchanged and calculate the variable cost per unit and the total fixed cost using the high/low technique.
- Adjustments may need to be made to the fixed costs when calculating the total cost for a new activity level.

Illustration 4 – the high/low method with stepped fixed costs

An organisation has the following total costs at three activity levels

Activity level (units)	4,000	6,000	7,500
Total cost	$40,800	$50,000	$54,800

Variable cost per unit is constant within this activity range and there is a step up of 10% in the total fixed costs when the activity level exceeds 5,500 units.

What is the total cost at an activity level of 5,000 units?

A $44,000

B $44,800

C $45,400

D $46,800

Solution

A

Calculate the variable cost per unit by comparing two output levels where fixed costs will be the same:

Variable cost per unit = [(54,800 – 50,000) ÷ (7,500 – 6,000)] = $3.20

Total fixed cost above 5,500 units = [54,800 – (7,500 × 3.20)] = $30,800

Total fixed cost below 5,500 units = 30,800/110 × 100 = $28,000

Total cost for 5,000 units = [(5,000 × 3.20) + 28,000] = $44,000

High/low method with changes in the variable cost per unit

Sometimes there may be changes in the variable cost per unit, and the high/low method can still be used to determine the fixed and variable elements of semi-variable costs. As with the stepped fixed costs – choose activity levels where the variable costs per unit remain unchanged.

Illustration 5 – The high/low method with changing variable costs

The following information relates to the manufacture of Product LL:

Output (units)	**Total cost** ($)
200	7,000
300	8,000
400	8,600

For output volumes above 350 units the variable cost per unit falls by 10%. (Note: this fall applies to all units – not just the excess above 350).

Required:

Estimate the cost of producing 450 units of Product LL.

Solution

$$\text{Variable cost per unit } (<350) = \frac{\$8{,}000 - \$7{,}000}{300 - 200} =$$

$$\frac{\$1{,}000}{100} = \$10 \text{ per unit}$$

Total cost at 300 units	=	$8,000
Total variable cost	= 300 × $10	$3,000
Therefore fixed cost	=	$5,000

If output is 450 units:

Variable cost	= 450 × $10 × 90%	$4,050
Fixed cost	=	$5,000
Total cost	=	$9,050

9 Cost equations

Cost equations are derived from historical cost data. Once a cost equation has been established, for example distinguishing the fixed and variable costs using the high/low method, it can be used to estimate future costs. Cost equations are assumed to have a linear function and therefore the equation of a straight line can be applied:

$y = a + bx$

Where:

- 'a' is the intercept, i.e. the point at which the line $y = a + bx$ cuts the y axis (the value of y when $x = 0$).
- 'b' is the gradient/slope of the line $y = a + bx$ (the change in y when x increases by one unit).
- 'x' = independent variable.
- 'y' = dependent variable (its value depends on the value of 'x').

This formula can be related to the results of the high/low calculation as follows:

- 'a' is the fixed cost per period (the intercept)
- 'b' is the variable cost per unit (the gradient)
- 'x' is the activity level (the independent variable)
- 'y' is the total cost = fixed cost + variable cost (dependent on the activity level)

Suppose a cost has a cost equation of y = \$5,000 + 10x, this can be shown graphically as follows:

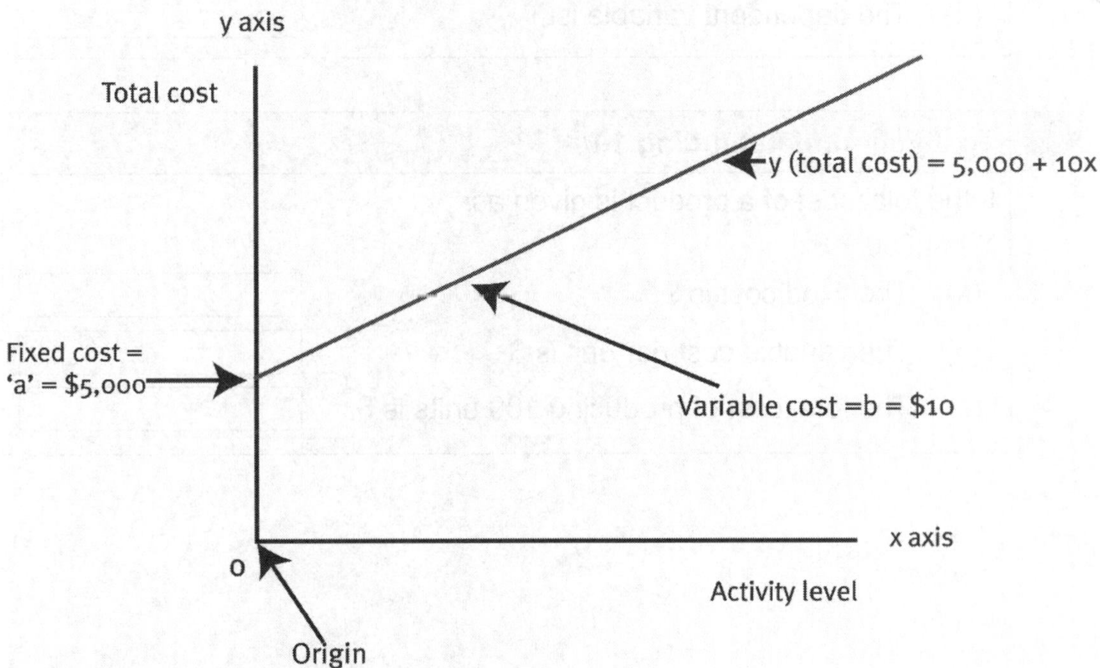

Illustration 6 – Cost equations

If y = 8,000 + 40x

(a) Fixed cost = $

(b) Variable cost per unit = $

(c) Total cost for 200 units = $

Solution

(a) Fixed cost = $ 8,000

(b) Variable cost per unit = $ 40

(c) Total cost for 200 units = $ 16,000

Working

Fixed cost = $8,000

Variable cost = 200 × $40 = $8,000

Total cost = fixed cost + variable cost = $8,000 + $8,000 = $16,000

Test your understanding 9

Consider the linear function y = 1,488 + 20x and answer the following questions.

(a) The line would cross the y axis at the point

(b) The gradient of the line is

(c) The independent variable is

(d) The dependent variable is

Test your understanding 10

If the total cost of a product is given as:

Y = 4,800 + 8x

(a) The fixed cost is $

(b) The variable cost per unit is $

(c) The total cost of producing 100 units is $

10 Cost codes

A code is a system of symbols designed to be applied to a classified set of items, to give a brief accurate reference, which helps entry into the records, collation and analysis.

A cost code is a code used in a costing system.

The first step in creating a cost code will be to determine the cost centre to which the cost relates and then to allocate the correct cost centre code.

Illustration 7 – Cost code example

If a cost relates to Machine Group 7 the cost centre code might be 07. If the cost relates to the canteen the cost centre code might be 16.

Generic or functional codes

Once a cost has been allocated its correct cost centre code then it may also be useful to know the particular type of expense involved. Therefore some more digits might be added to the cost centre code to represent the precise type of cost.

Illustration 8 – Generic or functional codes

If an expense for Machine Group 7 is for oil then its code might be 07 (for its cost centre) followed by 23 to represent indirect materials.

If an expense of the canteen is identified as frozen peas then its cost code might be 16 (its cost centre) followed by 02 to represent food purchases.

Specific codes

Finally it may be necessary for cost allocation, decision making or accounting purposes to allocate a code which specifically identifies the item of cost.

Illustration 9 – Specific codes example

The oil for Machine Group 7 might eventually be coded as 072304. This represents Machine Group 7 (07) indirect material use (23) of oil (04).

The frozen peas for the canteen might be coded as 160219. This represents canteen (16) food purchases (02) of frozen peas (19).

A cost code is designed to analyse and classify the costs of an organisation in the most appropriate manner for that organisation. Therefore there are no set methods of designing a cost code and the cost code of a particular organisation will be that which best suits the operations and costs of that business.

Test your understanding 11

A cost coding system is such that the first two letters of the code represent the cost centre, the third letter the type of expense and the fourth letter the detail of the expense.

Codes are as follows:

- S = Sales representative's expenses
- ED = Eastern Division
- P = Petrol

What is the correct code for an Eastern Division's sales representative's petrol expenses?

11 Coding systems

There are many ways to code costs. Here are some of the more popular methods:

Sequential code

This is the most basic type of code. It simply means that each code follows a numerical or alphabetical sequence. Planning is needed to determine how many codes might be needed in total.

For example, let's assume we are making a coding list for different types of expenses. We could give our first category, say Motor Expenses, code 001. Our next type of expense, say Electricity, would get code 002. Each expense would then follow in sequence. This allows us to have as many as 999 different types of expenses as we are using a three digit sequential code.

Block code

Block codes are often used to categorise sequential codes together. For example, an accounting system might have the following block codes:

Code	Item
0000	Expenses
1000	Revenue
2000	Non-current assets
3000	Current assets
4000	Long term liability
5000	Equity

The 3000 "Block" is allocated to Current assets. This means that it is possible to classify up to 1,000 different current assets (such as different types of inventories and bank accounts) using this block.

Hierarchical code

Each digit in the code represents a classification. As the code progresses from left to right each digit represents a smaller subset. For example, codes for sales for an international electronics retailer could have the hierarchy:

1 represents revenue

1.1 Revenue from the UK (.1)

1.2 Revenue from the USA (.2)

1.3 Revenue from China (.3)

This allows for infinite expandability. For example, it can be expanded as:

1.1.1 Revenue in the UK from laptop sales (.1)

1.1.2 Revenue in the UK from photocopier sales (.2)

1.2.1 Revenue in the USA from laptop sales (.1)

1.3.2 Revenue in China from photocopier sales (.2)

Each sub-category simply gets a further decimal coding.

Significant digit code

A significant digit code is a code that contains individual digits and letters that are used to represent features of the coded item. The example given is one used to describe packs of paper file dividers:

Code	Item
2000	Paper file dividers
2010	10 pack of paper file dividers
2020	20 pack of paper file dividers
2030	30 pack of paper file dividers

2000 is the code for the dividers and then the 10, 20, 30 represents the number of dividers in a pack.

Faceted code

A faceted code is one that is broken down into a number of facets or fields, each of which signifies a unit of information.

Consider the following simplified table which has been extracted as a sample from the faceted code used by a large international manufacturer:

Region	Code	Department	Code	Expense	Code
Europe	01	Sales	01	Salaries	0244
Asia	02	Production	02	National Insurance	0245
USA	03	Personnel and Finance	03	Pension contribution	0246
Africa	04	Administration	04	Bonus payments	0247

In this example, there are three facets, or fields, to the code:

Facet 1 is the region, and is 2 digits long

Facet 2 is the department, and is 2 digits long

Facet 3 is the type of expense, and is 4 digits long

If we wanted to post an expense for a bonus paid to the production department of the USA region, the code would be 03020247. That is: 03 (for USA), 02 (for Production) and 0247 (for Bonus payments).

It can be seen that a faceted system is a complicated one and requires lots of training and possibly a table such as the one above to be used for interpretation of codes. But it does allow for more sub-divisions and a greater number of codes.

Mnemonic code

Mnemonic means something that aids the memory or understanding. This uses an alphabetical coding rather than a numerical coding system. It is often used to abbreviate or simplify information.

For example, in accounting we might use:

Code	Meaning
NCA	Non-current assets
EXP	Expenses
REV	Revenue

Mnemonic codes are a way of quickly expressing information and making that information easily understood. However, this coding method makes it very difficult to use sub-categories or to have too much information. Mnemonic coding is likely to struggle to categorise 999 different types of expenses.

Test your understanding 12

Explain the following types of coding systems:

(a) sequence codes

(b) block codes

(c) significant digit codes

(d) faceted codes.

Test your understanding 13

A company operates from three main sites. In analysing its overhead costs it uses a nine-digit coding system. A sample from the coding manual shows:

Site	Code	Expenditure days	Code	Function	Code
Whitby	100	Rent	410	Purchasing	600
Scarborough	200	Power	420	Finance	610
York	300	Heat and light	430	Production	620
		Travel costs	500	Sales	630
		Telephone and postage	520		

The order of coding is: site/expense/function

An invoice for the York site for travel costs incurred by a sales representative would be coded as:

A 300/500/600

B 300/500/630

C 300/500/610

D 300/500/620

Test your understanding 14

The accounting system can contain codes to identify:

(i) the type of cost

(ii) the responsibility centre

(iii) the supplier.

Which of these options are correct?

A (i) only

B (ii) only

C (i) and (ii)

D (i), (ii) and (iii)

Test your understanding 15

An indirect cost should:

A be coded to a cost unit

B be coded to the different costs centres that incur the cost

C be coded to an overhead cost centre

D not be coded at all

12 Chapter summary

Cost object, cost unit and cost centre

Cost object – activity for which costs can be separately measured

Cost unit – unit of product or service in relation to which costs are ascertained

Cost centre – production or service location, function, activity or item of equipment for which costs can be ascertained

Production and non-production costs

Production costs = prime cost (total direct costs) plus overheads

Non-production costs = admin, selling, distribution and finance

Types of cost behaviour

Direct and indirect costs

Direct costs – directly involved in production

Indirect costs – not directly involved in production

Material, labour, overhead

Fixed and variable costs

Fixed – do not vary with level of activity

Variable – vary with level of activity

Analysis of semi-variable costs into fixed and variable elements

Cost equations
(linear function) y =a + bx

High/low analysis

$$\textbf{Variable cost per unit} = \frac{\text{Cost at high level of activity} - \text{Cost at low level of activity}}{\text{High level of activity} - \text{Low level of activity}}$$

Fixed cost = Total cost at activity level – Total variable cost

Test your understanding answers

Test your understanding 1

Cost	Materials, labour or expense	Direct or indirect
The hire of tools or equipment	Expense	Direct
Rent of a factory	Expense	Indirect
Supervisors' salaries	Labour	Indirect
Oil for lubricating machines	Material	Indirect
Wages of factory workers involved in production	Labour	Direct
Depreciation of equipment	Expense	Indirect

Test your understanding 2

(a) **B**

Store assistants are not directly involved in producing the output (goods or services) of an organisation.

(b) **B**

This is a basic definition question. Direct costs are costs which can be identified with a single cost unit, or cost centre.

Test your understanding 3

Cost	**Classification**
Overalls for machine workers	1
Cost of printer cartridges in general office	4
Salary of factory supervisor	1
Salary of payroll supervisor	4
Rent of warehouse for storing goods ready for sale	3
Loan interest	5
Salary of factory security guard	1
Early settlement discounts for customers who pay early	2
Salary of the Chairman's PA	4
Road tax licence for delivery vehicles	3
Bank overdraft fee	5
Salesmen's commissions	2

Test your understanding 4

The production cost includes:

	Per unit	Total
	$	$
Direct material cost	1	15,000
Direct labour cost	3	45,000
Variable production cost	3	45,000
Fixed production cost	2	30,000
	9	135,000

Test your understanding 5

The items of expenditure would be analysed as follows.

1	Fixed	5	Semi-variable
2	Fixed	6	Fixed
3	Variable	7	Stepped fixed
4	Semi-variable	8	Variable

Note: the depreciation charge for the factory machines (7) is a stepped fixed cost – when activity increases to such a level that a second and third machine is required, the fixed cost will step up.

Test your understanding 6

Total fixed cost is shown in graph	4
Total variable cost is shown in graph	1
Total semi-variable cost is shown in graph	3
Fixed cost per unit is shown in graph	6
Variable cost per unit is shown in graph	4
A stepped fixed cost is shown in graph	2

Test your understanding 8

The total costs incurred in 20X3 at various output levels in a factory have been measured as follows:

Output (units)	Total cost ($)
26	6,566
30	6,510
33	6,800
44	6,985
48	7,380
50	7,310

When output is 80 units or more, another factory unit must be rented and fixed costs therefore increase by 100%.

Variable cost per unit is forecast to rise by 10% in 20X4.

Required:

Calculate the estimated total costs of producing 100 units in 20X4.

Advantages and limitations of the high/low method

The main advantage of the high/low method is that it is easy to understand and easy to use.

The limitations of the high/low method are as follows:

- it relies on historical cost data and assumes this data can reliably predict future costs
- it assumes that activity levels are the only factor affecting costs
- it uses only two values (highest and lowest) to predict future costs and these results may be distorted because of random variations which may have occurred
- bulk discounts may be available for purchasing resources in large quantities.

Test your understanding 7

Variable cost per unit = $\frac{\$7,310 - \$6,566}{50 - 26} = \frac{\$744}{24}$ = \$31 per unit

Substituting at high activity level:

Total cost	=	\$7,310
Total variable cost	= 50 × \$31	\$1,550
Therefore fixed cost	=	\$5,760

Test your understanding 8

Variable cost per unit (20X3) = $\frac{\$7,310 - \$6,566}{50 - 26} = \frac{\$744}{24}$ = \$31 per unit

Substituting at high activity level:

Total cost	=	\$7,310
Total variable cost	= 50 × \$31	\$1,550
Therefore fixed cost	=	\$5,760

Estimated total costs of producing 100 units in 20X4:

Variable cost	= 100 × \$31 × 1.1	\$3,410
Fixed cost	= \$5,760 × 2	\$11,520
Total cost	=	\$14,930

Test your understanding 9

(a)	The line would cross the y axis at the point	1,488
(b)	The gradient of the line is	20
(c)	The independent variable is	x
(d)	The dependent variable is	y

Test your understanding 10

(a)	The fixed cost is $	4,800
(b)	The variable cost per unit is $	8
(c)	The total cost of producing 100 units is $	5,600

Working

Fixed cost = $4,800

Variable cost = 100 × $8 = $800

Total cost = fixed cost + variable cost = $4,800 + $800 = $5,600

Test your understanding 11

The code is:

EDSP

Test your understanding 12

(a) Sequence codes allocate a number, or a letter, to items in a simple list. Their main advantage lies in simplicity of allocation, but they provide no correlation between the items and their code numbers, and insertions and deletions are not so easily handled. It is much better to have the code progressing in groups of say 10 so that room is left for insertions.

(b) Block codes allocate bands of numbers to particular categories. With each category there is usually a limited amount of possible expansion. They have the merit of simplicity and give a more direct relationship between items and codes, which may help with indexing or information retrieval.

(c) Significant digit codes are when individual digits and letters are used to represent features of the coded item.

(d) Faceted codes are when the digits of the code are divided into facets of several digits and each facet represents some attribute of the item being coded. These codes are similar to significant digit codes but are purely numerical, which may be preferable in computer systems.

Test your understanding 13

B

300 for York followed by 500 for travel costs followed by 630 for the sales function.

Test your understanding 14

D

Codes representing the type of cost and responsibility centre will be used in the main ledger. The purchase ledger will contain codes representing individual suppliers so that details of supplier invoices and payments made to suppliers can be quickly accessed.

Test your understanding 15

C

It is more usual to code overhead costs to an overhead cost centre before sharing the costs to the cost centres that incur the cost.

Chapter

3

Accounting for materials

Chapter learning objectives

Upon completion of this chapter you will be able to:

- describe the different procedures and documents necessary for the ordering, receiving and issuing of materials from inventory
- identify, explain and calculate the costs of ordering and holding inventory (including buffer inventory)
- describe and apply appropriate methods for establishing reorder levels where demand in the lead time is constant
- calculate and interpret the optimal reorder quantities
- calculate and interpret the optimal reorder quantities when discounts apply
- produce calculations to minimise inventory costs when inventory is gradually replenished
- calculate the value of closing inventory and material issues using LIFO, FIFO and average methods
- describe the control procedures used to monitor physical and 'book' inventory and to minimise discrepancies and losses
- interpret the entries and balances in the material inventory account.

One of the PER performance objectives (PO1) is to take into account all relevant information and use professional judgement, your personal values and scepticism to evaluate data and make decisions. You should identify right from wrong and escalate anything of concern. You also need to make sure that your skills, knowledge and behaviour are up-to-date and allow you to be effective in your role. Working through this chapter should help you understand how to demonstrate that objective.

One of the PER performance objectives (PO12) is to apply different management accounting techniques is different business contexts to effectively manage and use resources. Working through this chapter should help you understand how to demonstrate that objective.

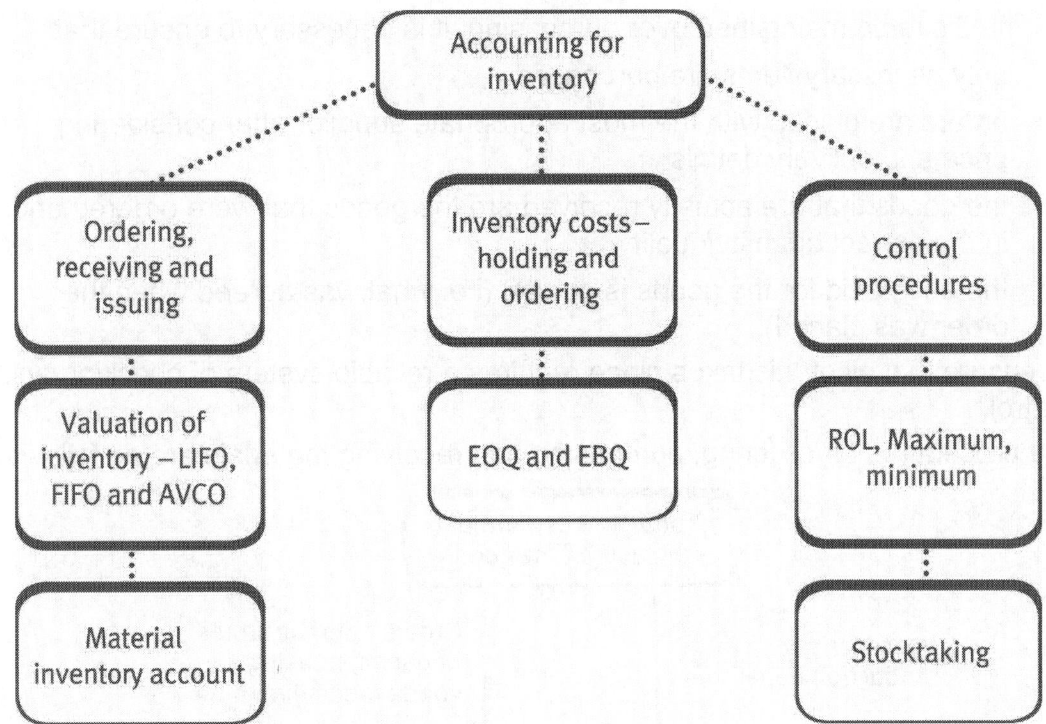

1 Ordering, receiving and issuing inventory

In a manufacturing business inventory (materials) may be the largest item of cost. The principal reasons why a business needs inventory are as follows:

- It acts as a buffer in times when there is an unusually high rate of consumption.
- It enables the business to take advantage of quantity discounts by buying in bulk.
- The business can take advantage of seasonal and other price fluctuations (e.g. an end of season sale).
- Any delay in production caused by lack of parts is kept to a minimum, so production processes will flow smoothly and efficiently.
- It may be necessary to hold inventory for a technical reason, for example, some food items need to 'mature'.

It is essential that the material purchased is the most suitable for the intended purpose. When material is required it must be ordered, received by the stores department, recorded, issued to the manufacturing department that requires it and eventually paid for. This process needs a great deal of paperwork and strict internal controls.

Internal control consists of full documentation and appropriate authorisation of all transactions, movements of materials and of all requisitions, orders, receipts and payments.

If control is to be maintained over purchasing, it is necessary to ensure that:

- only necessary items are purchased
- orders are placed with the most appropriate supplier after considering price and delivery details
- the goods that are actually received are the goods that were ordered and in the correct quantity/quality
- the price paid for the goods is correct (i.e. what was agreed when the order was placed).

To ensure that all of this takes place requires a reliable system of checking and control.

The procedures for ordering, purchasing and receiving materials are as follows:

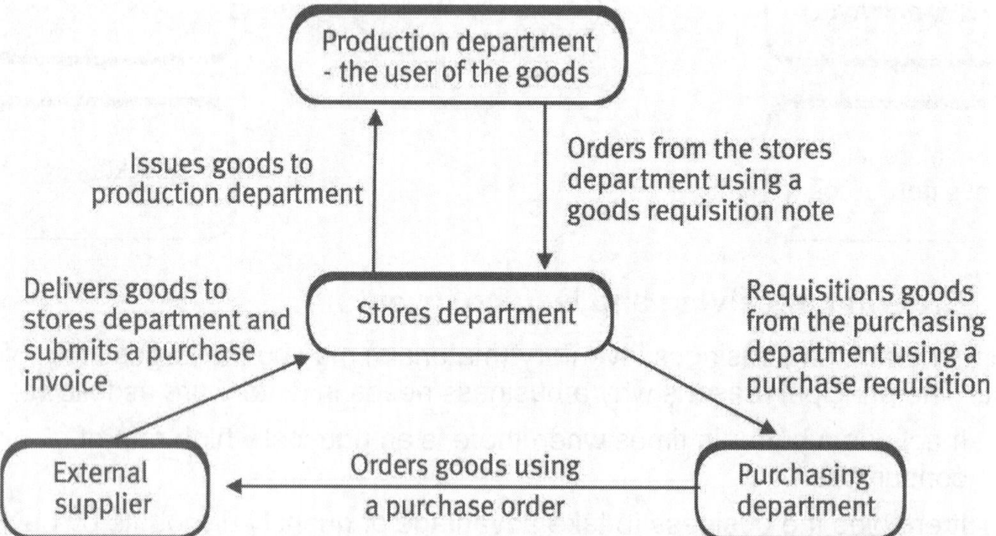

Notes for the diagram

- **Goods or Materials requisition notes** are issued by production departments. Their purpose is to authorise the storekeeper to release the goods which have been requisitioned. They may be used to update the stores records if the material is available for instant release.
- A **purchase requisition** is completed by the stores department (including authorisation by the relevant manager) and sent to the **purchasing department**.
- On receipt of a properly authorised requisition, the purchasing department will select a supplier and create an order on a **purchase order form**.
- The purchase order form is sent to the supplier and copies are also sent to the accounts department and the stores department.

- On receipt of the goods, the stores department will check the goods against the relevant purchase order, and check the **delivery note** which accompanies the goods. Full details of the goods are then entered onto a **goods received note (GRN)**.
- A copy of the GRN is attached to the relevant purchase order and they are both sent to the purchasing department where they are matched to the relevant supplier's purchase invoice. Once approved, the **purchase invoice** can be paid.

Other documentation a business may encounter include:

- **Materials returned notes** used to record any unused materials which are returned to stores.
- **Materials transfer notes** document the transfer of materials from one production department to another.
- **Goods returned notes** used to detail what is being returned to the supplier. The goods may be damaged or not as ordered.
- **Credit notes** are received if goods have been returned to the supplier or there is a fault with the invoice.

Specimen forms

PURCHASE REQUISITION

Date ....20...........   Serial No: ....

Purpose*: inventory/special
capital equipment/(budget reference)
*Delete as appropriate

Quantity and units	Description	Material code	Job or dept. code	Delivery required		Purchase order		
				Date	Place	No.	Date	Supplier

Origination department ....   Authorisation ....

PURCHASE ORDER

To: .... Serial No: ....

.... Date: ....

.... Purchase Req. No: ....

Please supply, in accordance with the attached conditions

Quantity	Description	Code	Delivery date	Price	Per

Your quotation ....

To be delivered, carriage paid, to .... Terms

Please quote our Purchase Order number on all correspondence.

For ABC Ltd

....

GOODS RECEIVED NOTE

To: .... Serial No: ....

.... Date issued: ....

Carrier: .... Purchase Order No: ....

Date of delivery: ....

Description	Code	Quantity	Packages	Gross Weight

INSPECTION REPORT			Received by: ....
Quantity passed	Quantity rejected	Remarks	Required by: ....
			Accepted: ....
Inspector .... Date			Date: ....

MATERIAL REQUISITION								
Charge job/ Cost Centre No:						Serial No: .... Date:		
Code No.	Description		Quantity or weight	Cost office only				
				Rate	Unit	$	$	Stores ledger
Authorised by:		Storekeeper:		Prices entered by:				
Received by:		Bin card entered:		Calculations checked:				

Test your understanding 1

A goods received note (GRN) provides (tick all that apply):

- [ ] Information used to update inventory records.
- [ ] Information to check that the correct price has been recorded on the supplier's invoice.
- [ ] Information to check that the correct quantity of goods has been recorded on the supplier's invoice.
- [ ] Information to record any unused materials which are returned to stores.

Test your understanding 2

The following documents are used within a cost accounting system:

(i) invoice from supplier

(ii) purchase order

(iii) purchase requisition

(iv) stores requisition

Which TWO of the documents are matched with the goods received note in the buying process?

A (i) and (ii)

B (i) and (iv)

C (ii) and (iii)

D (iii) and (iv)

Test your understanding 3

The following documents are used in accounting for raw materials:

(i) Goods received note

(ii) Materials returned note

(iii) Materials requisition note

(iv) Delivery note

Which of the documents can be used to update the stores ledger cards for inventory?

A (i) and (ii)

B (i) and (iv)

C (ii) only

D (ii) and (iii)

2 Inventory holding and ordering costs

Most businesses, whatever their size, will be concerned with the problem of which items to have in inventory and how much of each item should be kept.

Costs of carrying inventory

Irrespective of the nature of the business, a certain amount of inventory will need to be held.

However, holding inventory costs money and the principal 'trade-off' in an inventory holding situation is between the costs of acquiring and storing inventory and the level of service that the company wishes to provide.

The total cost of having inventory consists of the following:

- Purchase price
- Holding costs:
  - the opportunity cost of capital tied up
  - insurance
  - deterioration
  - obsolescence
  - damage and pilferage
  - warehouse upkeep
  - stores labour and administration costs.
- Ordering costs:
  - clerical and administrative costs – the total administrative costs of placing orders will increase in proportion to the number of orders placed. They therefore exhibit the behaviour of variable costs.
  - transport costs.
- Stock-out costs (items of required inventory are not available):
  - loss of sales
  - long-term damage to the business through loss of goodwill
  - production stoppages caused by a shortage of raw materials
  - extra costs caused by the need for emergency orders.
- Inventory recording systems costs:
  - maintaining the stores record card.

Costs of holding inventory

Holding costs can be distinguished between fixed holding costs and variable holding costs:

- Fixed holding costs include the cost of storage space and the cost of insurance. Note that the cost of storage space may be a stepped fixed cost if increased warehousing is needed when higher volumes of inventory are held.
- Variable holding costs include interest on capital tied up in inventory. The more inventory that is held, the more capital that is tied up.

Holding costs can be calculated as follows:

Total annual holding cost = holding cost per unit of inventory (Ch) × average inventory (Q/2).

Where average inventory held is equal to half of the order quantity Q.

Costs of ordering inventory

Ordering costs can be calculated as follows:

Total annual ordering cost = cost of placing an order (Co) × number of orders (D/Q).

Where the number of orders in a year is expected annual demand D divided by the order quantity Q.

Total annual cost of inventory

The Total Annual Costs (TAC) is the total of purchasing costs P multiplied by annual demand D plus total ordering costs (Co × D/Q) and total holding costs (Ch × Q/2):

Total annual cost = PD + (Co × D/Q) + (Ch × Q/2)

Costs of carrying buffer inventory

Buffer or safety inventory allows you to meet unpredictable peaks in demand, and it allows you to protect your customers from production breakdowns, supplier failures, or delays in deliveries from suppliers. It can also reduce the cost of purchasing as inventory levels should never get to a critical level.

However, buffer inventory ties up cash that could be better invested in other parts of the business. It costs money in terms of the opportunity cost (what else the cash could be being used for), the cost to insure the inventory, the cost to store the product, and the cost of theft or damage.

Buffer inventory could also end up being a huge liability if the demand falls or the product becomes obsolete before you can use the inventory.

Disadvantages of low and high inventory levels

Disadvantages of low inventory levels

To keep the holding costs low it may be possible to reduce the volume of inventory that is kept but this can cause some problems:

- Customer demand cannot always be satisfied; this may lead to loss of business if customers become dissatisfied.
- In order to fulfil commitments to important customers, costly emergency procedures (e.g. special production runs) may become necessary in an attempt to maintain customer goodwill.
- It will be necessary to place replenishment orders more frequently than if higher inventories were held, in order to maintain a reasonable service. This will result in higher ordering costs being incurred.

Disadvantages of high inventory levels

To reduce the problems mentioned above management may consider holding high levels of inventory but again this can have issues:

- Storage or holding costs are very high; such costs will usually include rates, rent, labour, heating, deterioration, etc.
- The cost of the capital tied up in inventories, i.e. the cash spent to buy the inventory is not available to pay other bills.
- If the stored product becomes obsolete, a large inventory holding of that item could, at worst, represent a large capital investment in an unsaleable product whose cash value is only that of scrap.
- If a great deal of capital is invested in inventory, there will be proportionately less money available for other requirements such as improvement of existing production facilities, or the introduction of new products.
- When a high inventory level of a raw material is held, a sudden drop in the market price of that material represents a cash loss to the business for having bought at the higher price. It follows that it would seem sensible to hold higher inventories during an inflationary period and lower inventories during a period of deflation.

Illustration 1 – The cost of holding inventory

A company uses components at the rate of 6,000 units per year, which are bought in at a cost of $1.20 each from the supplier. The company orders 1,000 units each time it places an order and the average inventory held is 500 units. It costs $20 each time to place an order, regardless of the quantity ordered.

The total holding cost is 20% per annum of the average inventory held.

Required

Calculate the annual ordering and holding costs

Solution

$$\text{Annual ordering cost} = \frac{\text{Annual usage}}{\text{Order size}} \times \$20$$

$$= \frac{6{,}000}{1{,}000} \times \$20$$

$$= \$120$$

Annual holding cost

= average inventory held x cost per unit × 20%

= 500 units × $1.20 × 20%

= $120

Test your understanding 4

A company has recorded the following details for Component 427 which is sold in boxes of 10 components.

Ordering cost	$32 per order placed
Purchase price	$20 per box of 10 components
Holding cost	10% of purchase price
Monthly demand	1,500 components

Component 427 is currently ordered in batches of 240 boxes at a time. The average inventory held is 120 boxes.

Required:

Calculate the annual holding cost and the annual ordering cost for Component 427.

3 Reorder levels

Reorder level

The reorder level is the quantity of inventory in hand when a replenishment order should be placed. It is calculated with reference to the time it will take to receive the order (the lead time) and the possible requirements during that time.

If the demand in the lead time is constant, the reorder level is calculated as follows:

Reorder level = Maximum usage × Maximum lead time

Illustration 2 – Reorder levels

A company uses Component M at the rate of 1,500 per week. The time between placing an order and receiving the components is five weeks. The reorder quantity is 12,000 units.

Required:

Calculate the reorder level.

Solution

Reorder level	= Usage × Lead time
	= 1,500 units × 5 weeks = 7,500 units

Test your understanding 5

A national chain of tyre fitters stocks a popular tyre for which the following information is available:

Usage – 175 tyres per day

Lead time – 16 days

Reorder quantity – 3,000 tyres

Based on the data above, at what level of inventory should a replenishment order be issued in order to ensure that there are no stock-outs?

A 2,240

B 2,800

C 3,000

D 5,740

4 The economic order quantity (EOQ)

The EOQ is the reorder quantity which minimises the total costs associated with holding and ordering inventory (i.e. holding costs + ordering costs) are at a minimum.

We can estimate the EOQ graphically by plotting holding costs, ordering costs and total costs against different levels of re-order quantities.

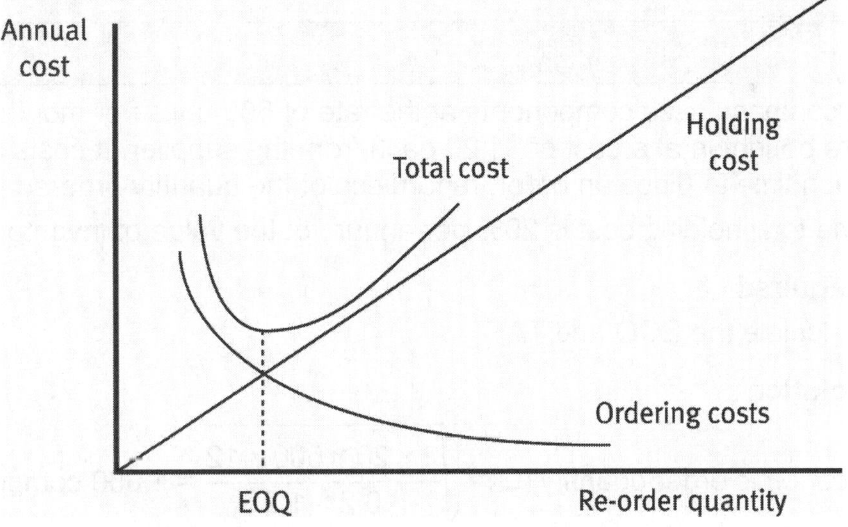

EOQ formula

The formula for the EOQ (or Q) is as follows:

$$Q = EOQ = \sqrt{\frac{2C_OD}{C_h}}$$ GIVEN

Where:

D = Demand per **annum**

C_o = Cost of placing **one** order

C_h = Cost of holding **one** unit for **one** year

Note that the formula for the EOQ is provided in your exam. You must make sure that you know what the different symbols represent so that you can use the formula correctly.

EOQ assumptions

There are a number of important assumptions related to the EOQ that you should note:

- Demand and lead time are constant and known
- Purchase price is constant
- No buffer inventory is held.

Illustration 3 – The economic order quantity (EOQ)

A company uses components at the rate of 500 units per month, which are bought in at a cost of $1.20 each from the supplier. It costs $20 each time to place an order, regardless of the quantity ordered

The total holding cost is 20% per annum of the value of inventory held.

Required

Calculate the EOQ and TAC

Solution

$$\text{Economic order quantity (Q)} = \sqrt{\frac{2 \times 20 \times 500 \times 12}{0.2 \times 1.2}} = 1{,}000 \text{ components}$$

Total annual cost = Purchase price × Annual Demand + (Cost of ordering × Annual Demand/Q) + (Cost of holding × Q/2)

$$TAC = (\$1.20 \times 500 \times 12) + \left(\$20 \times \frac{500 \times 12}{1{,}000}\right) + \left(\$1.20 \times 0.2 \times \frac{1{,}000}{2}\right) = \$7{,}440$$

Test your understanding 6

A company is planning to purchase 90,800 units of a particular item in the year ahead. The item is purchased in boxes each containing 10 units of the item, at a price of $200 per box. A safety inventory of 250 boxes is kept.

The cost of holding an item in inventory for a year (including insurance, interest and space costs) is 15% of the purchase price. The cost of placing and receiving orders is to be estimated from cost data collected relating to similar orders, where costs of $5,910 were incurred on 30 orders. It should be assumed that ordering costs change in proportion to the number of orders placed. 2% should be added to the above ordering costs to allow for inflation. Assume that usage of the item will be even over the year.

The order quantity which minimises total costs is [ ] boxes

5 The EOQ with discounts

Quantity discounts

It is often possible to negotiate a quantity discount on a purchase price offered by a supplier if bulk orders are placed.

If a quantity discount is accepted this will have the following effects:

- The annual purchase price will decrease.
- The annual holding cost will increase.
- The annual ordering cost will decrease.

EOQ when quantity discounts are available

The steps involved in calculating the EOQ when quantity discounts are available are as follows:

- Calculate the EOQ, ignoring discounts.

  If the EOQ is smaller than the minimum purchase quantity to obtain a bulk discount:
- calculate the total of the annual inventory holding costs, inventory ordering costs and inventory purchase costs at the EOQ.
- calculate the annual inventory holding costs, inventory ordering costs and inventory purchase costs quantity that qualifies for the bulk discount.
- compare the total costs and select the minimum cost alternative.
- If there is a further discount available for an even larger order size, repeat the same calculations for the higher discount level.

Illustration 4 – The EOQ with discounts

A company uses components at the rate of 500 units per month, which are bought in at a cost of $1.20 each from the supplier. It costs $20 each time to place an order, regardless of the quantity ordered.

The supplier offers a 5% discount on the purchase price for order quantities of 2,000 items or more. The current EOQ is 1,000 units.

The total holding cost is 20% per annum of the value of inventory held.

Required:

Should the discount be accepted?

Solution

Order quantity =	**1,000**		**2,000**
	$		$
Order cost			
(6,000/1,000 × $20)	120	(6,000/2,000 × $20) =	60
Holding cost			
(20% × $1.20 × 1,000/2)	120	($0.24 × 0.95 × 2,000/2) =	228
Purchase cost			
(6,000 × $1.20)	7,200	(6,000 × $1.20 × 0.95) =	6,840
Total annual costs	7,440		7,128

The discount should be accepted because it saves the company $312 ($7,440 – $7,128).

Test your understanding 7

Watton Ltd is a retailer of beer barrels. The company has an annual demand of 36,750 barrels. The barrels cost $12 each. Fresh supplies can be obtained immediately, but ordering costs and the cost of carriage inwards are $200 per order. The annual cost of holding one barrel in inventory is estimated to be $1.20. The economic order quantity has been calculated to be 3,500 barrels.

The suppliers introduce a quantity discount of 2% on orders of at least 5,000 barrels and 2.5% on orders of at least 7,500 barrels.

Required:

Determine whether the least-cost order quantity is still the EOQ of 3,500 barrels.

6 Gradual replenishment of inventory

Organisations who replenish inventory levels gradually by manufacturing their own products internally also need to calculate the most economical batch size to produce:

- The decisions faced by organisations that manufacture and store their own products involve deciding whether to produce large batches at long intervals OR produce small batches at short intervals.
- An amended EOQ model is used to help organisations to decide which course of action to take.
- The amended EOQ model is known as the Economic Batch Quantity (EBQ) model.
- As the items are being produced, there is a machine setup cost. This replaces the ordering cost of the EOQ.
- In the EOQ, inventory is replenished instantaneously whereas here, it is replenished over a period of time.
- Depending on the demand rate, part of the batch will be sold or used while the remainder is still being produced.

Large or small batches

- Producing large batches at long intervals will lead to low machine setup costs (as fewer machine setups will be needed) and high holding costs (high average inventory levels as more inventory held).
- Producing small batches at short intervals will lead to high machine setup costs (as more machine setups will be needed) and low holding costs (low average inventory levels as less inventory held).

The EBQ

The EBQ model is primarily concerned with determining the number of items that should be produced in a batch (compared to the size of an order with the EOQ).

The formula for the EBQ is as follows:

Economic batch quantity = $\sqrt{\dfrac{2C_oD}{C_h\left(1-\frac{D}{R}\right)}}$ GIVEN

Where:

Q = Batch size

D = Demand per **annum**

C_h = Cost of holding **one** unit for **one** year

C_o = Cost of setting up **one** batch ready to be produced

R = **Annual** replenishment rate

Illustration 5 – Gradual replenishment of inventory

The following is relevant for Item X:

- Production is at a rate of 500 units per week.
- Demand is 10,000 units per annum; evenly spread over 50 working weeks.
- Setup cost is $2,700 per batch.
- Storage cost is $2.50 per unit for a year.

Required:

Calculate the economic batch quantity (EBQ) for Item X.

Solution

Annual production rate, R = 500 × 50 = 25,000 units

Annual demand rate = 10,000 units

Cost per setup, C_o = $2,700

Cost of holding one item in inventory per year, C_h = $2.50

$$EBQ = \sqrt{\frac{2C_oD}{C_h\left(1-\left(\frac{D}{R}\right)\right)}} = \sqrt{\frac{2 \times 2{,}700 \times 10{,}000}{2.5\left(1-\frac{10{,}000}{25{,}000}\right)}} = 6{,}000 \text{ units}$$

Test your understanding 8

AB Ltd makes a component for one of the engines that it builds. It uses, on average, 2,000 of these components, steadily throughout the year. The component costs $16 per unit to make and it costs an additional $320 to setup the production process each time a batch of components is made. The holding cost per unit is 10% of the unit production cost.

The company makes these components at a rate of 200 per week, and the factory is open for 50 weeks per annum.

Required:

Calculate the EBQ.

Maximum and minimum inventory

Many inventory systems will also incorporate maximum and minimum inventory 'warning' levels, above or below which (respectively) inventory should not be allowed to rise or fall.

In practice, the maximum inventory level is fixed by taking into account:

- rate of consumption of the material
- time needed to obtain new supplies
- financial considerations due to high inventories tying up capital
- storage space with regard to the provision of space and maintenance costs
- extent to which price fluctuates
- risks of changing specifications
- possibility of loss by evaporation, deterioration, etc
- seasonal considerations as to both price and availability
- economic order quantities.

The minimum inventory level is fixed by taking into account:

- rate of consumption
- time needed to obtain delivery of supplies
- the costs and other consequences of stock-outs.

A simplified method of determining these control levels is by reference to the re-order level, re-order quantity and estimates of possible lead times and usage rates, as follows:

Minimum level = Re-order level – (Average usage × Average lead time)

Maximum level = Re-order level + Re-order quantity – (Minimum usage × Minimum lead time)

If at any time inventories fall below the minimum level, this is a warning that usage or lead time are above average. Thus the storekeeper will need to keep an eye on inventory levels and be prepared to place an emergency order if inventories get too low.

If inventories rise above the maximum level, then usage or lead time have actually been lower than the expected minimum. If it is usage, this may indicate a general decline in the demand for the inventory and the order quantity (and possibly the re-order level) should be reviewed to avoid holding excess inventory with associated holding costs.

7 Control procedures to minimise discrepancies and losses

The level of investment in inventory and the labour costs of handling and recording or controlling them is considerable in many organisations. It is for this reason that organisations must have control procedures in place in order to minimise discrepancies and losses.

Stocktaking

The process of stocktaking involves checking the physical quantity of inventory held on a certain date and then checking this balance against the balances on the stores ledger (record) cards or bin cards. Stocktaking can be carried out on a **periodic basis** or a **continuous basis**.

- **Periodic stocktaking** involves checking the balance of every item of inventory on the same date, usually at the end of an accounting period.
- **Continuous stocktaking** involves counting and valuing selected items of inventory on a rotating basis. Specialist teams count and check certain items of inventory on each day. Each item is checked at least once a year with valuable items being checked more frequently.
- Any differences (or discrepancies) which arise between 'book' inventory and physical inventory must be investigated.
- In theory any differences, as recorded in the stores ledger or the bin card, must have arisen through faulty recording.
- Once the discrepancy has been identified, the stores ledger card is adjusted in order that it reflects the true physical inventory count.
- Any items which are identified as being **slow-moving** or **obsolete** should be brought to the attention of management as soon as possible.
- Management will then decide whether these items should be disposed of and written off to the statement of profit or loss.
- Slow-moving items are those inventory items which take a long time to be used up.
- Obsolete items are those items of inventory which have become out of date and are no longer required.

Examples of other issues and controls

Issue	Control procedure
Ordering goods at inflated prices	• Use of standard costs for purchases • Quotation for special items
Fictitious purchases	• Separation of ordering and purchasing • Physical controls over materials receipts, usage and inventory
Shortages on receipts	• Checking in all goods inwards at gate • Delivery signatures
Losses from inventory	• Regular stocktaking • Physical security procedures
Writing off obsolete or damaged inventory which is good	• Control of responsible official over all write-offs
Losses after issue to production	• Records of all issues • Standard usage allowance

Inventory losses and waste

- Inventory losses may be quantified by comparing the physical quantity of an item held with the balance quantity recorded on the bin card and/or stores ledger card.
- There are two categories of loss: those which occur because of theft, pilferage, damage or similar means and those which occur because of the breaking of bulk receipts into smaller quantities.
- It is the second of these which are more commonly referred to as waste.
- Inventory losses must be written off against profits as soon as they occur. If the value to be written off is significant then an investigation should be made of the cause.
- When waste occurs as a result of breaking up bulk receipts, it is reasonable to expect that the extent of such wastage could be estimated in advance based upon past records. Either of two accounting treatments could then be used:
  - Issues continue to be made and priced without any adjustment and the difference at the end of the period is written off.
  - Alternatively, the issue price is increased to compensate for the expected waste.

- Suppose that a 100 metre length of copper is bought for $99. The estimated loss caused by cutting into shorter lengths as required is 1%.
- The issue price could be based on the expected issues of 99 metres, i.e. $1 per metre rather than pricing the copper at:

  Issue price= $\frac{\$99}{100}$ = $0.99/metre

8 Valuing inventory

Perpetual inventory

Perpetual inventory is the recording as they occur of receipts, issues and the resulting balances of individual items of inventory in either quantity or quantity and value.

- Inventory records are updated using stores ledger cards and bin cards.
- Bin cards also show a record of receipts, issues and balances of the quantity of an item of inventory handled by stores.
- As with the stores ledger card, bin cards will show materials received (from purchases and returns) and issued (from requisitions).
- A typical stores ledger card is shown below.

STORES LEDGER CARD								
Description:		Unit:		Location:		Code:		
Maximum:		Minimum:		Reorder level:		Reorder quantity:		
Receipts			Issues			On order		
Date/ref	Quantity	$	Date/ref	Quantity	$	Date/ref	Quantity	$

Inventory valuation is important for:

- Financial reporting
  - for inclusion in the Financial statements of a business
- Costing
  - to calculate how much to charge for a product based on the amount of inventory consumed.

To charge units of inventory with an appropriate value the business will consistently use an appropriate basis:

- FIFO (First In First Out)
- LIFO (Last In First Out)
- AVCO or WACO (Weighted Average Cost)

All will be illustrated using following information.

Illustration 6 – Inventory valuation

M Ltd had the following material transactions during the first week in March.

		Quantity (units)	**Unit cost** $
Opening balance	1st March	10	2.00
Receipts	2nd March	70	2.20
Issues	3rd March	40	
Receipts	4th March	50	2.30
Issues	5th March	70	

Note: per unit prices are rounded to 2 decimal places and total figures are to the nearest whole number.

FIFO

- Assumes that materials are issued out of inventory in the order in which they were delivered into inventory.
- Appropriate for many businesses (e.g. retailer selling fresh food using sell-by date rotation techniques).

Illustration 7 – FIFO inventory valuation

Date	Receipts			Issues			Balance		
	Units	*Unit cost* $	*Total cost* $	*Units*	*Unit cost* $	*Total cost* $	*Units*	*Unit cost* $	*Total cost* $
Op/Bal							10	2.00	20
2nd Mar	70	2.20	154				10	2.00	20
							70	2.20	154
									174
3rd Mar				10	2.00	20	40	2.20	88
				30	2.20	66			
				40		86			
4th Mar	50	2.30	115				40	2.20	88
							50	2.30	115
									203
5th Mar				40	2.20	88	20	2.30	46
				30	2.30	69			
				70		157			

- Closing inventory valuation = Opening inventory + receipts – issues

  = $20 + ($154 + $115) – ($86 + $157) = $46

Features of FIFO

Advantages:	**Disadvantages:**
• Logical – reflects the most likely physical flow. • Easily understood. • Inventory values at up-to-date prices. • Acceptable to HM Revenue and Customs and IAS2.	• Issues may be at out-of-date prices. • In times of rising prices reported profits are high ('high' closing inventory valuations). • Cost comparisons between jobs are difficult.

LIFO

- Assumes that materials are issued out of inventory in the reverse order to which they were delivered. An uncommon method which is only appropriate for a few businesses
  - e.g. a coal merchant who stores coal inventories in a large 'bin'.

Illustration 8 – LIFO inventory valuation

Date	Receipts			Issues			Balance		
	Units	*Unit cost* ($)	*Total cost* ($)	*Units*	*Unit cost* ($)	*Total cost* ($)	*Units*	*Unit cost* ($)	*Total cost* ($)
Op/Bal							10	2.00	20
2nd Mar	70	2.20	154				10 70	2.00 2.20	20 154 ——— 174
3rd Mar				40	2.20	88	10 30	2.00 2.20	20 66 ——— 86
4th Mar	50	2.30	115				10 30 50	2.00 2.20 2.30	20 66 115 ——— 201

5th Mar				50	2.30	115	10	2.00	20
				20	2.20	44	10	2.20	22
				——		——			——
				70		159			42

- Closing inventory valuation = Opening inventory + receipts – issues
  $20 + ($154 + $115) – ($88 + $159) = $42

Features of LIFO

Advantages:	**Disadvantages:**
• Issue prices are up-to-date. • In times of rising prices, reported profits are reduced (as in this example where closing inventory is valued at 'lower' cost).	• Not usually acceptable to the HM Revenue & Customs and accounting standards. • Inventory values may become very out-of-date. • Cost comparisons between jobs are difficult.

AVCO

- All issues and inventory are valued at an average price.
- The average price is recalculated after each receipt.
- Cumulative weighted average price = $\frac{\text{Total costs before issue}}{\text{Total number of units before issue}}$
- Could be appropriate for businesses such as an oil merchant, where deliveries are fully mixed in with existing inventory.

Illustration 9 – AVCO inventory valuation

Date	Receipts			Issues			Balance		
	Units	*Unit cost* ($)	*Total cost* ($)	*Units*	*Unit cost* ($)	*Total cost* ($)	*Units*	*Unit cost* ($)	*Total cost* ($)
Op/Ball							10	2.00	20
2nd Mar	70	2.20	154				80	2.18	174
3rd Mar				40	2.18	87	40		87

4th Mar	50	2.30	115				90	2.24	202
5th Mar				70	2.24	157	20		45

- AVCO price after 2nd March delivery
  = ($20 + $154)/(10 + 70) = $174/80 = $2.18 per unit
- Closing inventory valuation = Opening inventory + receipts – issues
  = $20 + ($154 + $115) – ($87 + $157) = $45

Features of AVCO

Advantages:	**Disadvantages:**
• Acceptable to Accounting Standards and HM Revenue & Customs. • Logical because units all have the same value.	• Issue prices and inventory values may not be an actual purchase price (as in above example). • Inventory values and issue prices may both lag behind current values (e.g. issue on 5 March is at $2.244/unit whereas most recent purchase price = $2.30/unit).

The following information relates to TYUs 9 to 12.

A business had opening inventory of 300 units valued at $4.50 per unit on 1 May. The following receipts and issues were recorded in May:

2 May	Issue	200 units
7 May	Receipt	500 units @ $4.80 per unit
13 May	Issue	400 units
20 May	Receipt	500 units @ $5.00 per unit
28 May	Issue	450 units

Test your understanding 9

What is the value of issues during the month using the FIFO method?

A $4,750

B $5,000

C $5,030

D $5,080

Test your understanding 10

What is the value of issues during the month using the LIFO method?

A $4,750

B $5,000

C $5,030

D $5,070

Test your understanding 11

What is the value of closing inventory?

	FIFO method	LIFO method
A	$1,180	$1,250
B	$1,250	$1,180
C	$1,250	$730
D	$1,180	$730

Test your understanding 12

What is the value of closing inventory using the AVCO method? (per unit values to 2 decimal places)

A $1,180

B $1,231

C $1,250

D $1,282

9 Accounting for inventory – the material inventory account

Material inventory account

Materials held in store are an asset and are recorded as inventory in the statement of financial position of a company.

Accounting transactions relating to materials are recorded in the material inventory account.

Material inventory account

Debit entries reflect an **increase** in inventory	Credit entries reflect a **decrease** in inventory
• purchases	• issues to production
• returns to stores	• returns to suppliers

Illustration 10 – Accounting for inventory

Material inventory account

	$000		$000
Opening balance (1)	33	Work-in-progress (4)	137
Payables (2)	146	Materials returned to suppliers (5)	2
		Production overhead account (6)	4
Materials returned to stores (3)	4		
		Statement of profit or loss (7)	3
		Closing balance (8)	37
	183		183

1 The opening balance of materials held in inventory at the beginning of a period is shown as a debit in the material inventory account.

2 Materials purchased on credit are debited to the material inventory account.

3 Materials returned to stores cause inventory to increase and so are debited to the material inventory account.

4 **Direct** materials used in production are transferred to the **work-in-progress** account by crediting the material inventory account.

5 Materials returned to suppliers cause inventory levels to fall and are therefore 'credited out' of the material inventory account.

6 **Indirect** materials are not a direct cost of manufacture and are treated as **overheads**. They are therefore transferred to the production overhead account by way of a credit to the material inventory account.

7 Any material write-offs are 'credited out' of the material inventory account and transferred to the statement of profit or loss where they are written off.

8 The balancing figure on the material inventory account is the closing balance of material inventory at the end of a period. It is also the opening balance at the beginning of the next period.

Test your understanding 13

Transaction	Debit which account?	Credit which account?
Issue materials to production.		
Purchase new materials on credit.		
Materials returned to store from production.		
Materials written off.		
Indirect materials transferred to production overheads.		

10 Chapter summary

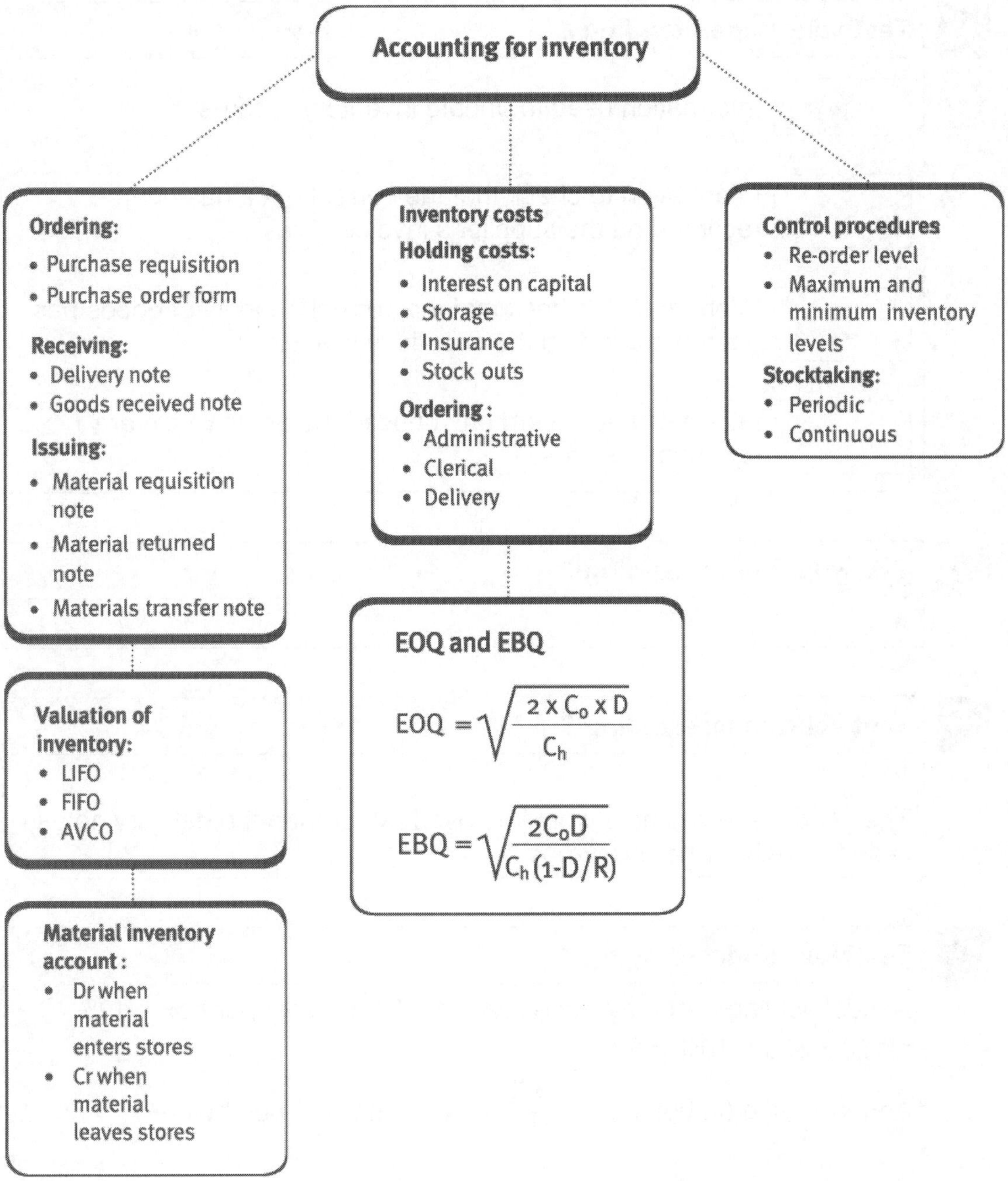

Accounting for inventory

Ordering:
- Purchase requisition
- Purchase order form

Receiving:
- Delivery note
- Goods received note

Issuing:
- Material requisition note
- Material returned note
- Materials transfer note

Valuation of inventory:
- LIFO
- FIFO
- AVCO

Material inventory account:
- Dr when material enters stores
- Cr when material leaves stores

Inventory costs

Holding costs:
- Interest on capital
- Storage
- Insurance
- Stock outs

Ordering:
- Administrative
- Clerical
- Delivery

EOQ and EBQ

$$EOQ = \sqrt{\frac{2 \times C_o \times D}{C_h}}$$

$$EBQ = \sqrt{\frac{2C_oD}{C_h(1-D/R)}}$$

Control procedures
- Re-order level
- Maximum and minimum inventory levels

Stocktaking:
- Periodic
- Continuous

Test your understanding answers

Test your understanding 1

✓	Information used to update inventory records.
	Information to check that the correct price has been recorded on the supplier's invoice.
✓	Information to check that the correct quantity of goods has been recorded on the supplier's invoice.
	Information to record any unused materials which are returned to stores.

Test your understanding 2

A

Test your understanding 3

A

The goods received note would be used rather than the delivery note in case the delivery note is wrong.

Test your understanding 4

Annual holding cost = average inventory held × cost per box × 10%

= 120 × \$20 × 10% = \$240

Annual usage (in boxes) = $\frac{1,500}{10}$ × 12 months = 1,800 boxes

Annual ordering cost = $\frac{\text{Annual usage}}{\text{Order size}}$ × \$32

= $\frac{1,800}{240}$ × \$32

= \$240

Test your understanding 5

B

Reorder level = Usage × Lead time

= 175 × 16

= 2,800 units

Test your understanding 6

The order quantity which minimises total costs is **349 boxes**

Working

To avoid confusion this question is best tackled by working in boxes not units.

C_o =	5,910/30	× 1.02	= $200.94
C_h =	0.15	× $200	= $30 per box
D =	90,800/10		= 9,080 boxes
EOQ	$\sqrt{(2 \times 200.94 \times 9,080/30)}$		= 349 boxes

Test your understanding 7

Order size	3,500 barrels	5,000 barrel	7,500 barrels
Purchase cost	36,750 × $12 = $441,000	36,750 × $12 × 98% = $432,180	36,750 × $12 × 97.5% = $429,975
Holding cost	$1.20 × 3,500/2 = $2,100	$1.20 × 5,000/2 = $3,000	$1.20 × 7,500/2 = $4,500
Ordering cost	$200 × 36,750/3,500 = $2,100	$200 × 36,750/5,000 = $1,470	$200 × 36,750/7,500 = $980
Total cost	$445,200	$436,650	$435,455

Total costs are minimised with an order size of 7,500 barrels.

Test your understanding 8

D		= 2,000 units
R	= 200 × 50	= 10,000 units
C_o		= \$320
C_h	= 10% of \$16	= \$1.60

$$EBQ = \sqrt{\frac{2C_oD}{C_h\left(1-\frac{D}{R}\right)}} = \sqrt{\frac{2\times320\times2{,}000}{1.60\ (1-2{,}000/10{,}000)}} = 1{,}000 \text{ units}$$

Test your understanding 9, 10 and 11

TYU 9 B, TYU 10 D, TYU 11 B

Workings

FIFO

Date	Receipts			Issues			Balance		
	Units	*Unit cost* (\$)	*Total cost* (\$)	*Units*	*Unit cost* (\$)	*Total cost* (\$)	*Units*	*Unit cost* (\$)	*Total cost* (\$)
Op/Ball							300	4.50	1,350
2nd May				200	4.50	900	100	4.50	450
7th May	500	4.80	2,400				100	4.50	450
							500	4.80	2,400
							600		2,850
13th				100	4.50	450	200	4.80	960
				300	4.80	1,440			
				400		1,890			
20th	500	5.00	2,500				200	4.80	960
							500	5.50	2,500
							700		3,460
28th				200	4.80	960	250	5.00	**1,250**
				250	5.00	1,250			
				450		2,210			

Total cost of FIFO issues = \$900 + \$1,890 + \$2,210 = \$5,000

LIFO

Date	Receipts			Issues			Balance		
	Units	*Unit cost* ($)	*Total cost* ($)	*Units*	*Unit cost* ($)	*Total cost* ($)	*Units*	*Unit cost* ($)	*Total cost* ($)
Op/Ball							300	4.50	1,350
2nd May				200	4.50	900	100	4.50	450
7th May	500	4.80	2,400				100	4.50	450
							500	4.80	2,400
							600		2,850
13th				400	4.80	1,920	100	4.50	450
							100	4.80	480
							200		930
20th	500	5.00	2,500				100	4.50	450
							100	4.80	480
							500	5.50	2,500
							700		3,430
28th May				450	5.00	2,250	100	4.50	450
							100	4.80	480
							50	5.00	250
							250		**1,180**

Total cost of LIFO issues = $900 + $1,920 + $2,250 = $5,070

Test your understanding 12

B

Date	Receipts			Issues			Balance		
	Units	*Unit cost* ($)	*Total cost* ($)	*Units*	*Unit cost* ($)	*Total cost* ($)	*Units*	*Unit cost* ($)	*Total cost* ($)
Op/Ball							300	4.50	1,350
2nd May				200	4.50	900	100	4.50	450
7th May	500	4.80	2,400				100 500 600	4.50 4.80	450 2,400 2,850
13th				400	4.75	1,900	200		950
20th	500	5.00	2,500				200 500 700	 5.00	950 2,500 3,450
28th May				450	4.93	2,219	250	5.00	**1,231**

Test your understanding 13

Transaction	**Debit which account?**	**Credit which account?**
Issue materials to production.	Work-in-progress	Material inventory account.
Purchase new materials on credit.	Material inventory account.	Payables
Materials returned to store from production.	Material inventory account.	Work-in-progress account.
Materials written off.	Statement of profit or loss.	Material inventory account.
Indirect materials transferred to production overheads.	Production overhead account.	Material inventory account.

Chapter

4

Accounting for labour

Chapter learning objectives

Upon completion of this chapter you will be able to:

- calculate direct and indirect costs of labour
- explain the methods used to relate input labour costs to work done
- prepare the journal and ledger entries to record labour costs inputs and outputs
- interpret entries in the labour account
- describe different remuneration methods: time-based systems; piecework systems and individual and group incentive schemes
- calculate the level, and analyse the costs and causes of labour turnover
- explain and calculate labour efficiency, capacity and production volume ratios.

PER

One of the PER performance objectives (PO12) is to apply different management accounting techniques is different business contexts to effectively manage and use resources. Working through this chapter should help you understand how to demonstrate that objective.

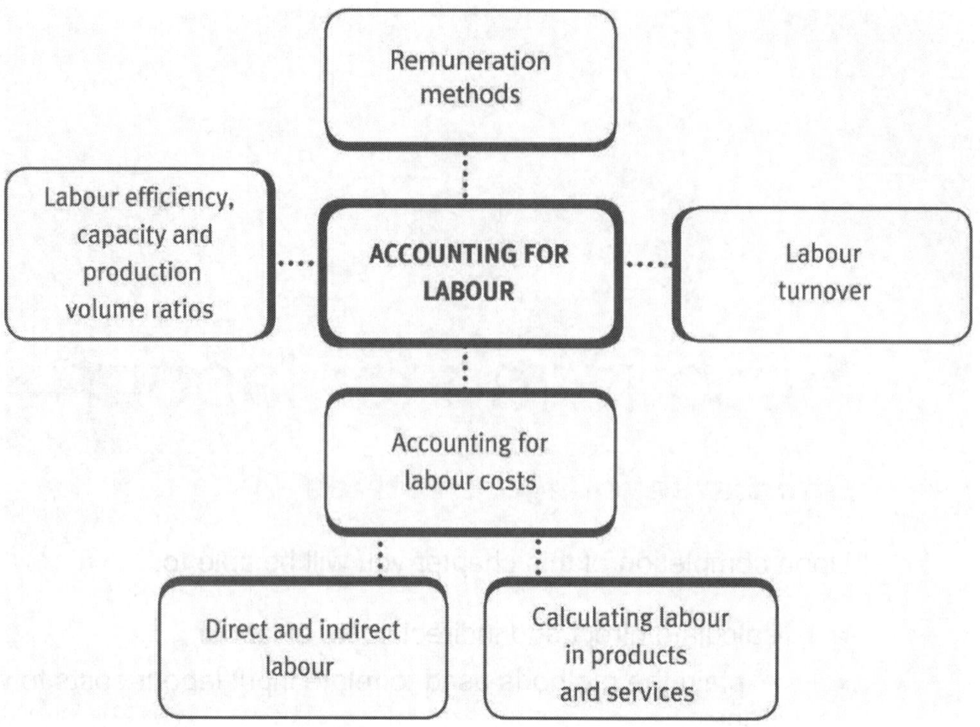

1 Remuneration methods

Payroll department

The payroll department is involved in carrying out functions that relate input labour costs to the work done.

- Preparation of the payroll involves calculating gross wages from time and activity records.
- The payroll department also calculates net wages after deductions from payroll.
- The payroll department also carries out an analysis of direct wages, indirect wages, and cash required for payment.

There are two basic approaches to remuneration – time-related or output-related.

Time-related systems

The most common remuneration method is to calculate pay or wages based on the number of hours an employee works.

- Employees are paid a basic rate per hour, day, week or month.
- Time-based systems do not on the whole provide any incentive for employees to improve productivity and close supervision is often necessary.
- Overtime can be paid at a premium if any extra hours are worked. Overtime is looked at in more detail in section 3.
- The formula for a time-based system is as follows.

Total wages = (total hours worked × basic rate of pay per hour) + (overtime hours worked × overtime premium per hour)

- A guaranteed minimum wage is often required due to minimum wage requirements.

Methods for recording the length of time an employee spends working can include:

- time sheets
- time cards
- job sheets.

Time records

It is essential that organisations employ relevant methods in both manufacturing and service industries to relate the labour costs incurred to the work done. One of the ways in which this can be done is to make records of the time spent by employees doing jobs.

- Time recording is required both for payment purposes and also for determining the costs to be charged to specific jobs.
- In many manufacturing industries employees will be supplied with an attendance record on which to record their time of arrival and departure from the factory. Such records are known as time cards (gate or clock cards) and are used to calculate wages and rates of pay.
- Plastic 'swipe' cards directly linked to a central computer can also be used.

Activity time records

Another method of relating work done to costs incurred is by the use of activity time records. Activity time records may be either period related or task related.

- Period-related timesheets are commonly used in service industries, for example in accountancy firms where time spent working for different clients is analysed, often to the nearest 15 minutes.
- Period-related timesheets are records that may cover days, weeks or sometimes longer periods.
- Task related activity time records are known as job sheets, operations charts or piecework tickets. They are generally more accurate and reliable than time-related activity time records, and are essential when incentive schemes are in use.

An example of a daily timesheet is illustrated on the next page.

Time Sheet					
Employee name:			No:		
Start date:			Finish date:		
Department:			Operation:		
Day	Start	Finish	Time	Production	Supervisor's signature
1					
2					
3					
4					
5					
Total Time allowed Time saved					
			Hours	Rate $	Paid $
Time wages Bonus Total wages					

Output related systems

A **piecework** system pays a fixed amount per unit produced. The formula for a piecework system is as follows.

Total wages = (units produced × rate of pay per unit)

- A guaranteed minimum wage is often required due to minimum wage requirements.
- Piecework is often combined with a time-based system to provide an added incentive to employees.

Types of piecework system

There are two main piecework systems that you need to know about:

- **Straight piecework systems** – the same rate per unit is paid no matter how many units are produced. These systems are almost extinct today as employees are more likely to be paid a guaranteed minimum wage within a straight piecework system.
- **Differential piecework systems** – these systems are the most widely used piecework systems and involve different piece rates for different levels of production.

Illustration 1 – Piecework schemes

A company operates a piecework system of remuneration, but also guarantees its employees 75% of a time-based rate of pay which is based on \$19 per hour for an eight hour working day. Each unit should take 3 minutes to produce (standard time). Employees are paid based on the number of hours their output should have taken (standard hours). Piecework is paid at the rate of \$18 per standard hour.

If an employee produces 200 units in eight hours on a particular day, what is the employee gross pay for that day?

Solution

200 units × standard time of 3 minutes per unit = 600 minutes, or 10 hours.

Employee gross pay = 10 hours × \$18 = \$180

Guaranteed (\$19 × 8 hours) × 75% = \$152 × 75% = \$114

As gross pay exceeds the guaranteed amount, the answer is \$180.

Test your understanding 1

The following graph shows the wages earned by an employee during a single day.

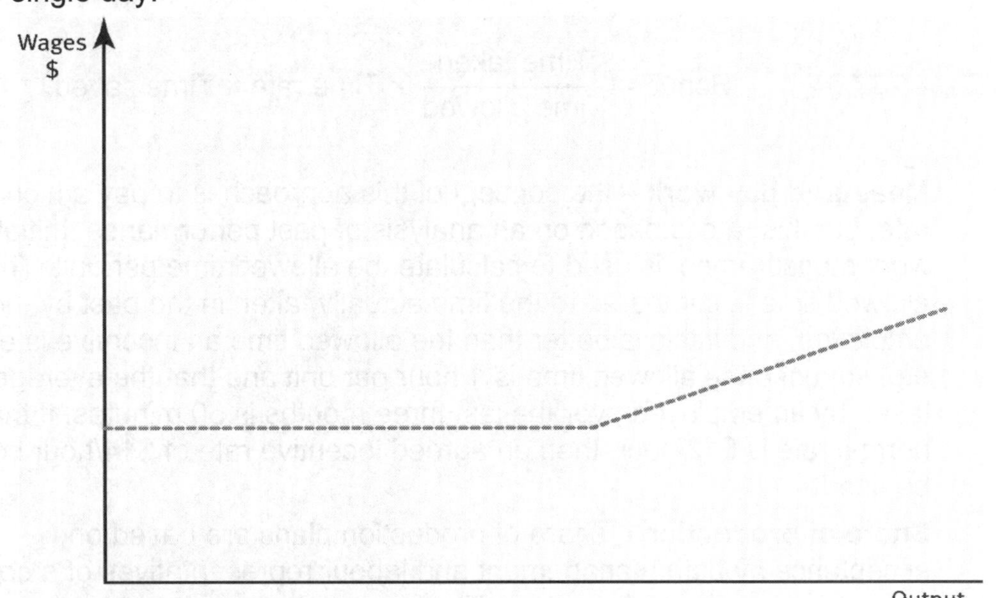

Which one of the following remuneration systems does the graph represent?

A Differential piecework

B A flat rate per hour with a premium for overtime working

C Straight piecework

D Piecework with a guaranteed minimum daily wage

2 Incentive schemes

Incentive schemes can be aimed at individuals and/or groups.

- Many different systems exist in practice for calculating bonus schemes. General rules are as follows:
  - They should be closely related to the effort expended by employees.
  - They should be agreed by employers/employees before being implemented.
  - They should be easy to understand and simple to operate.
  - They must be beneficial to all of those employees taking part in the scheme.
- Most bonus schemes pay a basic time rate, plus a portion of the time saved as compared to some agreed allowed time. These bonus schemes are known as **premium bonus plans**. For example:
  - The employee receives 50% of the time saved.

$$\text{Bonus} = \frac{\text{Time allowed} - \text{Time taken}}{2} \times \text{Time rate}$$

  - The proportion paid to the employee is based on the ratio of time taken to time allowed.

$$\text{Bonus} = \frac{\text{Time taken}}{\text{Time allowed}} \times \text{Time rate} \times \text{Time saved}$$

- **Measured day work** – the concept of this approach is to pay a high time rate, but this rate is based on an analysis of past performance. Initially, work measurement is used to calculate the allowed time per unit. This allowed time is compared to the time actually taken in the past by the employee, and if this is better than the allowed time an incentive is agreed, e.g. suppose the allowed time is 1 hour per unit and that the average time taken by an employee over the last three months is 50 minutes. If the normal rate is $12/hour, then an agreed incentive rate of $14/hour could be used.
- **Share of production** – share of production plans are based on acceptance by both management and labour representatives of a constant share of value added for payroll. Thus, any gains in value added – whether by improved production performance or cost savings – are shared by employees in this ratio.

Illustration 2 – Incentive schemes

The following data relate to Job A.

Employee's basic rate = $4.80 per hour

Allowed time for Job A = 1 hour

Time taken for Job A = 36 minutes

The employee is paid the basic rate for the allowed time for the job and then the bonus based on any time saved. The bonus is calculated based on the following formula:

$$\text{Bonus} = \frac{\text{Time taken}}{\text{Time allowed}} \times \text{Time rate} \times \text{Time saved}$$

Required

Calculate the total payment for Job A

Solution

		$
Bonus	$= \frac{36}{60} \times \frac{\$4.80}{60} \times 24$	1.15
Basic rate	=	4.80
Total payment for Job A		5.95

Test your understanding 2

Ten employees work as a group. When production of the group exceeds the standard – 200 pieces per hour – each employee in the group is paid a bonus for the excess production in addition to wages at hourly rates.

The bonus is computed thus: the percentage of production in excess of the standard quantity is found, and one half of the percentage is regarded as the employees' share. Each employee in the group is paid as a bonus this percentage of a wage rate of $5.20 per hour. There is no relationship between the individual worker's hourly rate and the bonus rate.

The following is one week's record:

	Hours worked	Production
Monday	90	24,500
Tuesday	88	20,600
Wednesday	90	24,200
Thursday	84	20,100
Friday	88	20,400
Saturday	40	10,200
	480	120,000

During this week, Jones worked 42 hours and was paid $3 per hour basic.

Complete the following.

1 The bonus rate for the week was $ ☐

2 The total bonus for the group for the week was $ ☐

3 The total pay for Jones for the week was $ ☐

In the examination you will be given clear instructions on any bonus scheme in operation. You should follow the instructions given carefully in order to calculate the bonus payable from the data supplied

3 Direct and indirect labour

One of the most important distinctions of labour is between **direct** and **indirect** costs.

- Direct labour costs make up part of the prime cost of a product and include the basic pay of direct workers.
- Direct workers are those employees who are directly involved in producing the output of the business.
- Indirect labour costs make up part of the overheads (indirect costs) and include the basic pay of indirect workers.
- Indirect workers are those employees who are **not** directly involved in producing the output of the business, (for example, maintenance staff, factory supervisors and canteen staff).
- Indirect labour costs also include the following:
  - Bonus payments.
  - Benefit contributions.
  - Idle time (when workers are paid but are not making any products, for example when a machine breaks down).
  - Sick pay.
  - Time spent by direct workers doing 'indirect jobs' for example, cleaning or repairing machines.

Test your understanding 3

Which one of the following should be classified as direct labour?

A Supervisors' salaries in a factory

B Maintenance workers looking after equipment in a hospital

C Bricklayers in a house building company

D Wages of cleaning and housekeeping personnel

Overtime and overtime premiums

If employees are entitled to extra pay when hours in excess of contracted hours are worked then they will be paid for **overtime**. When employees work overtime, they receive an **overtime payment** which includes a **basic pay** element and an **overtime premium**.

- For example, if Fred is paid a basic wage of $8 per hour and overtime is paid at time and a half, when Fred works overtime, he will receive an overtime payment of $12 per hour ($8 basic + $4 premium (50% × $8)).

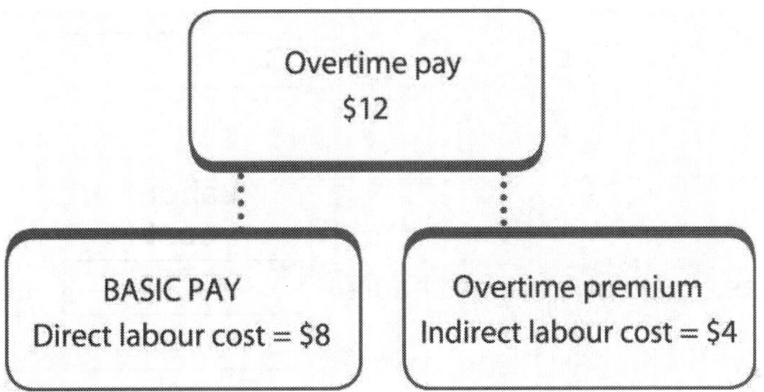

It is important that the overtime payment is analysed correctly into direct and indirect labour costs.

- Basic pay (whether it relates to overtime or normal working hours) is always classified as a direct labour cost for direct labour workers.
- Overtime premiums are usually classified as an indirect labour cost but if the extra hours are at the **specific request of a customer** because they want a job to be finished as soon as possible they can be classified as direct labour.
- Employees who work night shifts, or other anti-social hours may be entitled to a shift allowance or shift premium. Shift premiums are similar to overtime premiums where the extra amount paid above the basic rate is treated as an indirect labour cost.

Illustration 3 – Direct and indirect labour

Vienna is a direct labour employee who works a standard 35 hours per week and is paid a basic rate of $12 per hour. Overtime is paid at time and a third. In week 8 she worked 42 hours and received a $50 bonus.

Required

Calculate the following labour costs and state if it is a direct or indirect cost:

	Labour cost	Direct or Indirect
Basic pay for standard hours	$	
Basic pay for overtime hours	$	
Overtime premium	$	
Bonus	$	

Solution

		Labour cost	Direct or Indirect
1	Basic pay for standard hours	$420	Direct
2	Basic pay for overtime hours	$84	Direct
3	Overtime premium	$28	Indirect
4	Bonus	$50	Indirect

Workings:

1 Basic pay for standard hours = 35 hours × $12 per hour = $420

Basic pay for standard hours is a **direct labour cost** because the work involved is directly attributable to production.

2 Basic pay for overtime hours = 7 hours × $12 = $84. This is also a **direct labour cost** because the **basic rate for overtime** is part of the direct labour cost. It is the **overtime premium** which is usually part of the indirect labour cost.

3 Overtime premium = 1/3 of $12 = $4

Total overtime premium = 7 hours × $4 = $28

Unless overtime is worked at the specific request of a customer, overtime premium is part of the **indirect labour costs** of an organisation

Test your understanding 4

A company operates a factory which employed 40 direct workers throughout the four-week period just ended. Direct employees were paid at a basic rate of $4.00 per hour for a 38-hour week. Total hours of the direct workers in the four-week period were 6,528. Overtime, which is paid at a premium of 35%, is worked in order to meet general production requirements. Employee deductions total 30% of gross wages. 188 hours of direct workers' time were registered as idle.

Calculate the direct and indirect costs for the four-week period just ended.

Direct labour cost	$
Indirect labour cost	$

4 Accounting for labour costs

Labour costs are recorded in an organisation's statement of profit and loss. Accounting transactions relating to labour are recorded in the labour account.

- The labour account is debited with the labour costs incurred by an organisation. The total labour costs are then analysed into direct and indirect labour costs.
- **Direct labour costs** are credited from the labour account and debited in the work-in-progress (WIP) account. Remember, direct labour is directly involved in production and are therefore transferred to WIP before being transferred to finished goods and then cost of sales.
- **Indirect labour costs** are credited from the labour account and debited to the production overheads account. It is important that total labour costs are analysed into their direct and indirect elements.

Illustration 4 – Accounting for labour costs

Labour account

	$000		$000
Bank (1)	80	WIP (2)	60
		Production overheads (3)	
		Indirect labour	14
		Overtime premium	2
		Shift premium	2
		Sick pay	1
		Idle time	1
	80		80

1 Labour costs incurred are paid out of the bank before they are analysed further in the labour account.

2 The majority of the labour costs incurred by a manufacturing organisation are in respect of direct labour costs. Direct labour is directly involved in production and the cost incurred is transferred out of the labour account via a credit entry, to the WIP account.

3 Indirect labour costs include indirect labour (costs of indirect labour workers), overtime premium (unless overtime is worked at the specific request of a customer), shift premium, sick pay and idle time. All of these indirect labour costs are collected in the production overheads account. They are transferred there via a credit entry out of the labour account and then debited in the production overheads account.

Test your understanding 5

The following information is taken from the payroll records of a company.

	Direct workers	Indirect workers	Total
	$	$	$
Basic pay for basic hours	43,000	17,000	60,000
Overtime – basic pay	10,000	4,500	14,500
Overtime – premium	5,000	2,250	7,250
Training	2,500	1,250	3,750
Sick pay	750	250	1,000
Idle time	1,200	–	1,200

Required:

Using the information given, complete the labour account shown below:

Labour account

	$000		$000
	———		———
	———		———

5 Labour turnover

Labour turnover is a measure of the proportion of people leaving relative to the average number of people employed.

- Management might wish to monitor labour turnover, so that control measures might be considered if the rate of turnover seems too high.
- Labour turnover is calculated for any given period of time using the following formula:

$$\frac{\textbf{Number of leavers who require replacement}}{\textbf{Average number of employees}} \times 100$$

Illustration 5 – Labour turnover

At 1 January a company employed 3,641 employees and at 31 December employee numbers were 3,735. During the year 624 employees chose to leave the company.

Required

What was the labour turnover rate for the year?

Solution

Labour turnover rate =

$$\frac{\text{Number of leavers who require replacement}}{\text{Average number of employees}} \times 100$$

Average number of employees in the year = (3,641 + 3,735) ÷ 2 = 3,688.

$$\text{Labour turnover rate} = \frac{624}{3{,}688} \times 100\% = 16.9\%$$

Test your understanding 6

A company had 4,000 staff at the beginning of 20X8. During the year, there was a major restructuring of the company and 1,500 staff were made redundant and 400 staff left the company to work for one of the company's main competitors. 400 new staff joined the company in the year to replace those who went to work for the competitor.

Required:

Calculate the labour turnover rate for 20X8.

Causes and costs of labour turnover

Causes

It is important to try to identify why people leave an organisation and to distinguish between avoidable and unavoidable causes of labour turnover.

- Causes of labour turnover – avoidable:
  - poor remuneration
  - poor working conditions
  - lack of training opportunities
  - lack of promotion prospects
  - bullying in the workplace.
- Causes of labour turnover – unavoidable:
  - retirement
  - illness/death
  - family reasons (e.g. pregnancy)
  - relocation.
- Efficient managers will investigate high levels of labour turnover and aim to keep that turnover rate at a minimum.

Costs

Every time an employee leaves, an organisation will incur costs that are associated with replacing the employee. These costs are known as replacement costs.

- Replacement costs include the following:
  - advertising costs
  - cost of selection (time spent interviewing etc.)
  - training new employees
  - reduced efficiency until the new employee reaches the required skill.

- A high labour turnover rate tends to lower the performance of employees who remain in the organisation. Such employees may become restless and resentful of the extra burden of training new members and of additional temporary duties imposed upon them.
- In order to keep the labour turnover rate to a minimum, organisations should aim to prevent employees from leaving. Such preventive measures come with their own costs, known as preventive costs.
- Preventive costs include the costs associated with escaping the avoidable causes of labour turnover:
  - pay competitive wages and salaries if remuneration is poor
  - improve poor working conditions
  - offer good training opportunities
  - make sure promotion prospects arise as necessary
  - stamp out bullying in the workplace
  - investigate high labour turnover rates objectively.

6 Labour efficiency, capacity and production volume ratios

Labour efficiency ratio

Labour is a significant cost in many organisations and it is important to continually measure the efficiency of labour against pre-set targets.

- The labour efficiency ratio measures the performance of the workforce by comparing the actual time taken to do a job with the expected or standard time.
- The standard time is how long it should take to complete the actual output.
- The labour efficiency ratio is calculated using the following formula:

$$\frac{\textbf{Standard hours for actual output}}{\textbf{Actual hours worked to produce output}} \times 100$$

Idle time ratio

Sometimes the workforce is 'idle' through no fault of its own, and cannot get on with productive work. This happens if machines break down, or needs to be reset for a new production run. An idle time ratio can be calculated as follows:

$$\frac{\textbf{Idle hours}}{\textbf{Total hours}} \times 100$$

Labour capacity ratio

The labour capacity ratio measures the number of hours spent actively working as a percentage of the total hours available for work (full capacity or budgeted hours). The labour capacity ratio is calculated using the following formula:

$$\frac{\textbf{Actual hours worked to produce output}}{\textbf{Total budgeted hours}} \times 100$$

Labour production volume ratio ('activity' ratio)

- The labour production volume ratio compares the number of hours expected to be worked to produce actual output with the total hours available for work (full capacity or budgeted hours).
- The labour production volume ratio is calculated using the following formula:

$$\frac{\textbf{Standard hours for actual output}}{\textbf{Total budgeted hours}} \times 100$$

Illustration 6 – Labour efficiency, capacity and production volume ratios

A company budgets to make 800 units in 400 hours in a period.

Actual output during the period was 840 units which took 410 hours to make.

Required

Calculate the labour efficiency, capacity and production volume ratios.

Solution

Standard hours = 400 hours/800 units = 0.5 hours per unit.

Standard hours for actual output = 840 units × 0.5 hours per unit = 420 standard hours

Labour efficiency ratio:

$$\frac{\text{Standard hours for actual output}}{\text{Actual hours worked to produce output}} \times 100\%$$

$$= 420/410 \times 100\% = 102\%$$

Labour capacity ratio:

$$\frac{\text{Actual hours worked to produce actual output}}{\text{Total budgeted hours}} \times 100\%$$

$$= 410/400 \times 100\% = 102.5\%$$

Production volume ratio:

$$\frac{\text{Standard hours for actual output}}{\text{Total budgeted hours}} \times 100\%$$

$$= 420/400 \times 100\% = 105\%$$

Test your understanding 7

A company budgets to make 40,000 units of Product DOY in 4,000 hours in a year.

Actual output during the year was 38,000 units which took 4,180 hours to make.

Required:

Calculate the labour efficiency, capacity and production volume ratios.

7 Chapter summary

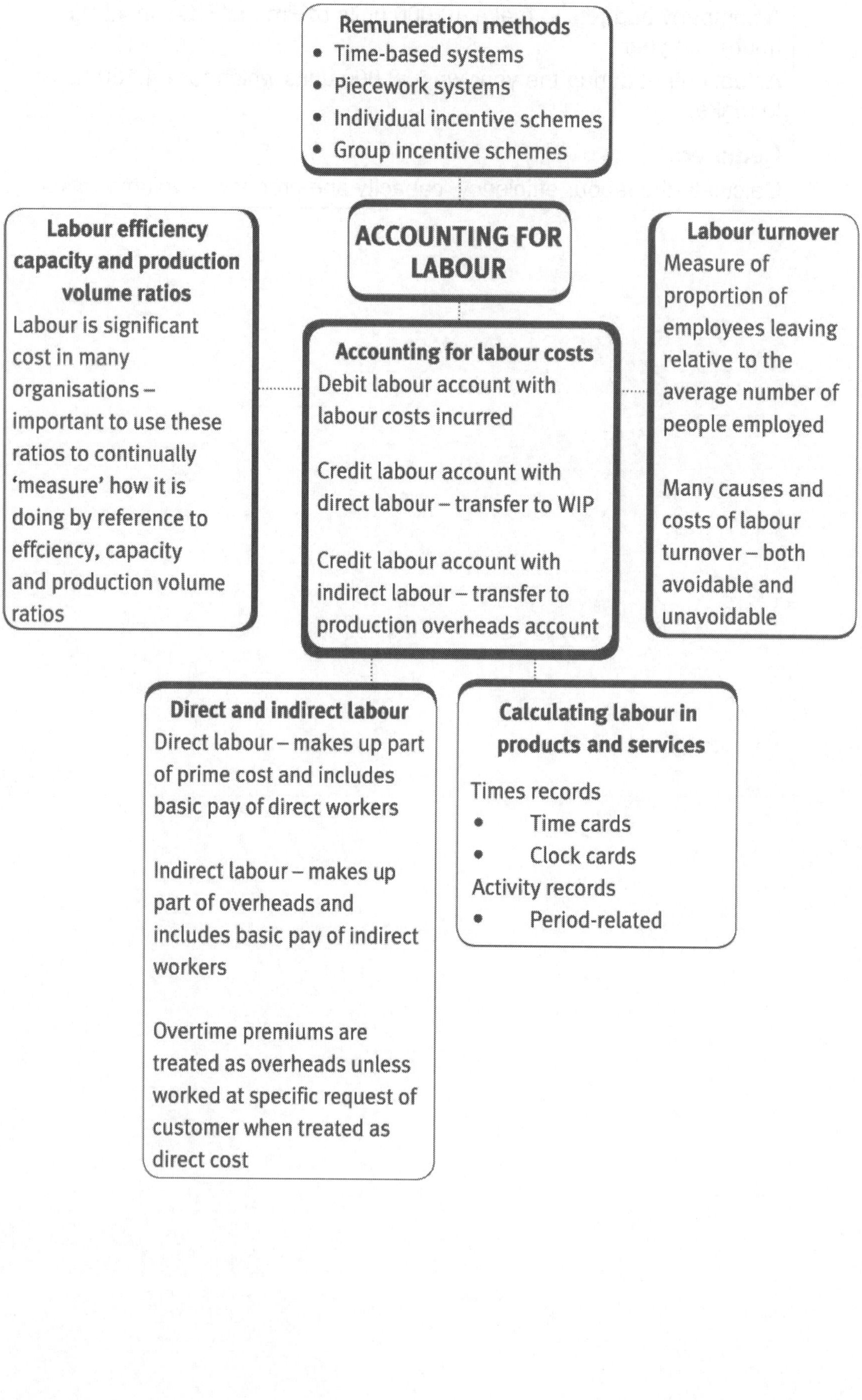

Remuneration methods
- Time-based systems
- Piecework systems
- Individual incentive schemes
- Group incentive schemes

ACCOUNTING FOR LABOUR

Labour efficiency capacity and production volume ratios
Labour is significant cost in many organisations – important to use these ratios to continually 'measure' how it is doing by reference to effciency, capacity and production volume ratios

Accounting for labour costs
Debit labour account with labour costs incurred

Credit labour account with direct labour – transfer to WIP

Credit labour account with indirect labour – transfer to production overheads account

Labour turnover
Measure of proportion of employees leaving relative to the average number of people employed

Many causes and costs of labour turnover – both avoidable and unavoidable

Direct and indirect labour
Direct labour – makes up part of prime cost and includes basic pay of direct workers

Indirect labour – makes up part of overheads and includes basic pay of indirect workers

Overtime premiums are treated as overheads unless worked at specific request of customer when treated as direct cost

Calculating labour in products and services

Times records
- Time cards
- Clock cards

Activity records
- Period-related

Test your understanding answers

Test your understanding 1

D

The graph represents a piecework system (as shown by the gentle upward-sloping line) with a guaranteed minimum daily wage (as shown by the horizontal line).

Test your understanding 2

1	The bonus rate for the week was $	0.65
2	The total bonus for the week was $	312
3	The total pay for Jones for the week was $	153.30

Workings

Standard production for the week = 480 hours × 200 = 96,000 pieces

Actual production for the week = 120,000 pieces

Excess production = 120,000 – 96,000 = 24,000

1 Bonus rate = 24,000 ÷ 96,000 × 0.5 × $5.20
= $0.65 per hour

2 Total bonus = 480 hours × $0.65
= $312

3 Pay for Jones = 42 × (3.00 + 0.65)
= $153.30

Test your understanding 3

C

Test your understanding 4

Direct labour cost	$25,360
Indirect labour cost	$1,379.20

Workings

Basic time	= 40 workers × 38 hrs/week × 4 weeks	= 6,080 hrs
Overtime	= Total time – Basic time	
	= 6,528 – 6,080	= 448 hrs
Productive time	= Total time – Idle time	
	= 6,528 – 188	= 6,340 hrs
Direct labour	= 6,340 hours at $4.00 per hour	= $25,360
Indirect labour	= Overtime premium + Idle time costs	
	= (448 hours × $4.00 × 35%) + (188 hours × $4.00/hr)	= $1,379.20

Test your understanding 5

Labour account

	$		$
Bank	87,700	WIP (43,000 + 10,000)	53,000
		Production overheads	
		Indirect labour (17,000 + 4,500)	21,500
		Overtime premium	7,250
		Training	3,750
		Sick pay	1,000
		Idle time	1,200
	87,700		87,700

Test your understanding 6

Number of staff at beginning of year = 4,000

Number of staff at end of year = 4,000 – 1,500 – 400 + 400 = 2,500

Labour turnover rate =

$$\frac{\text{Number of leavers who require replacement}}{\text{Average number of employees}} \times 100$$

$$\text{Average number of employees in the year} = \frac{4{,}000 + 2{,}500}{2} = 3{,}250$$

$$\text{Labour turnover rate} = \frac{400}{3{,}250} \times 100\% = 12.3\%$$

Test your understanding 7

Standard hours for actual output = 38,000 × 0.1 hours = 3,800 standard hours.

Labour efficiency ratio:

$$\frac{\text{Standard hours for actual output}}{\text{Actual hours worked to produce output}} \times 100\%$$

$$= (3{,}800/4{,}180) \times 100\% = 91\%$$

Labour capacity ratio:

$$\frac{\text{Actual hours worked to produce output}}{\text{Total budgeted hours}} \times 100\%$$

$$= (4{,}180/4{,}000) \times 100\% = 104.5\%$$

Production volume ratio:

$$\frac{\text{Standard hours for actual output}}{\text{Total budgeted hours}} \times 100\%$$

$$= \frac{3{,}800}{4{,}000} \times 100\% = 95\%$$

Chapter

5

Accounting for overheads

Chapter learning objectives

Upon completion of this chapter you will be able to:

- explain the different treatment of direct and indirect expenses
- describe the procedures involved in determining production overhead absorption rates
- allocate and apportion production overheads to cost centres using an appropriate basis
- reapportion service cost centre costs to production cost centres (including using the reciprocal method where service cost centres work for each other)
- select, apply and discuss appropriate bases for absorption rates
- prepare journal and ledger entries for manufacturing overheads incurred and absorbed
- calculate and explain the under and over absorption of overheads.

PER

One of the PER performance objectives (PO12) is to apply different management accounting techniques is different business contexts to effectively manage and use resources. Working through this chapter should help you understand how to demonstrate that objective.

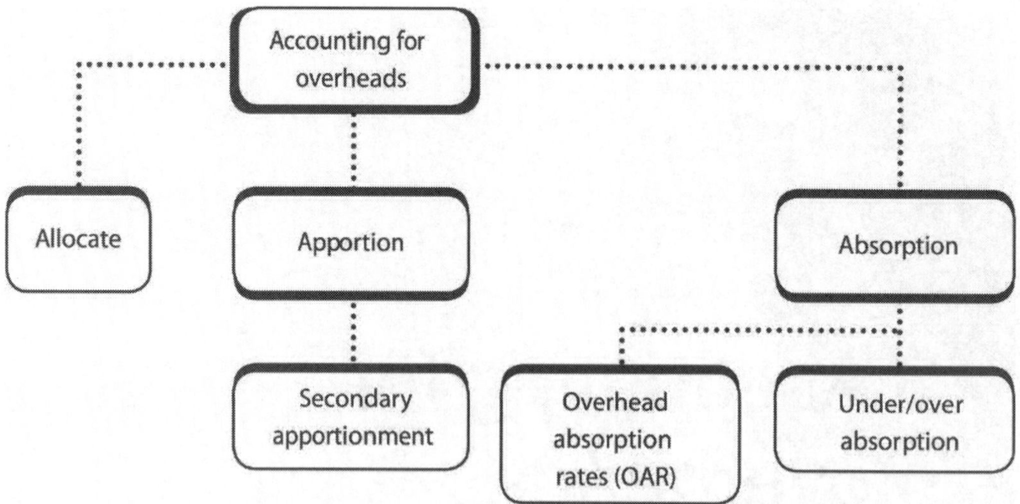

1 Direct and indirect expenses

Direct expenses are expenses that **can** be directly identified with a specific cost unit or cost centre.

- There are not many examples of direct expenses but royalties paid to a designer or fees paid to a subcontractor for a specific job could be classed as direct expenses.
- Direct expenses, direct materials and direct labour are the **prime** cost of a product.

Indirect expenses are expenses that **cannot** be directly identified with a specific cost unit or cost centre.

- The cost of renting a factory is classified as an indirect cost as the rent could be covering the manufacturing location of all products and also possibly other areas of the business such as the accounting department, a non-production location. It is not possible to relate the rent to a single products or location.
- Indirect expenses, indirect materials and indirect labour are the **overheads** of a business.

2 Production (manufacturing) overheads

Overheads can be grouped based on where in the business they are incurred:

- Production/manufacturing
- Administration
- Sales and distribution.

This chapter focuses on how production overheads are absorbed into the products being manufactured.

Production overheads of a factory can include the following costs:

- heating the factory
- lighting the factory
- renting the factory.

Production may take place over a number of different production cost centres and each cost centre should be assigned with its fair share of overhead cost. Examples of production cost centres include:

- Assembly
- Machining
- Finishing.

There may also be a number of production service cost centres that provide support to the production cost centres. Examples of production service cost centres include:

- Maintenance
- Canteen
- Stores.

Absorption costing

Production overheads are recovered by absorbing them into the cost of a product and this process is called absorption costing.

- The main aim of absorption costing is to recover overheads in a way that fairly reflects the amount of time and effort that has gone into making a product or service.
- Absorption costing involves the following stages:
  - allocation and apportionment of overheads to the different production cost centres
  - reapportionment of production service cost centre overheads to the production cost centres
  - absorption of overheads into the products.
- Absorption costing allows businesses to make decisions about pricing policies and value its inventory in accordance with IAS 2.

IAS 2

IAS 2 *Inventories* defines cost as comprising: 'all costs of purchase, costs of conversion and other costs incurred in bringing the inventories to their present location and condition'.

Specifically excluded are:

(a) abnormal amounts of wasted materials, labour and other production costs

(b) storage costs, unless necessary in the production process before a further production stage

(c) administrative overheads that do not contribute to bringing inventories to their present location and condition

(d) selling costs.

3 Allocation and apportionment

Allocation and apportionment of overheads

The first stage of the absorption costing process involves the allocation and apportionment of overheads.

- Allocation involves charging overheads directly to specific cost centres (production and/or service).
- If overheads relate to more than one production or service cost centre, then they must be shared between these cost centres using a method known as apportionment.
- Overheads must be apportioned between different production and service cost centres on a fair basis.

Bases of apportionment

There are no hard and fast rules for which basis of apportionment to use except that whichever method is used to apportion overheads, it must be fair. Possible bases of apportionment include the following:

- floor area – for rent and rates overheads
- carrying amount of non-current assets – for depreciation and insurance of machinery
- number of employees – for canteen costs.

Illustration 1 – Allocation and apportionment

LS Ltd has two production cost centres (Assembly and Finishing) and two production service cost centres (Maintenance and Canteen).

The following are budgeted costs for the next period:

Indirect materials	– $20,000
Rent	– $15,000
Electricity	– $10,000
Machine depreciation	– $5,000
Indirect labour	– $16,520

The following information is available:

	Assembly	**Finishing**	**Maintenance**	**Canteen**	**Total**
Area (sq metres)	1,000	2,000	500	500	4,000
kW hours consumed	2,750	4,500	1,975	775	10,000
Machine value($)	45,000	35,000	11,000	9,000	100,000
Staff	18	30	12	2	62
Direct labour hours	3,175	3,800	–	–	6,975
Indirect materials budget ($)	7,000	8,000	3,000	2,000	20,000
Indirect labour budget ($)	1,600	2,220	11,200	1,500	16,520

Required:

Complete the extract from the overhead analysis sheet shown below.

Solution

(W1) Indirect materials are allocated directly to the relevant cost centres.

(W2) Rent is apportioned to all cost centres based on the area occupied.

Total rent cost	= $15,000
Total area occupied	= 4,000 sq metres
Apportioned to Assembly cost centre	= area of assembly/total area × cost = 1,000/4,000 × $15,000 = $3,750

(W3) Electricity is apportioned to all cost centres on the basis of kW hours.

Total electricity costs	= $10,000
Total kW hours consumed	= 10,000 kW hours
Apportioned to Finishing cost centre	= 4,500/10,000 × $10,000 = $4,500

(W4) Machine depreciation is apportioned to all cost centres on the basis of machine value.

Total machine depreciation costs = $5,000

Total machine value = $100,000

Apportioned to Maintenance cost centre = 11,000/100,000 × $5,000 = $550

(W5) Indirect labour costs are allocated directly to all cost centres based on the indirect labour budget for each cost centre.

Overhead analysis sheet

Overhead	*Basis of apportionment*	*Assembly* $	*Finishing* $	*Maintenance* $	*Canteen* $	*Total* $
Indirect materials	Allocated (W1)	7,000	8,000	3,000	2,000	20,000
Rent	Area (W2)	3,750	7,500	1,875	1,875	15,000
Electricity	kW Hours (W3)	2,750	4,500	1,975	775	10,000
Machine depreciation	Machine value (W4)	2,250	1,750	550	450	5,000
Indirect labour	Allocated (W5)	1,600	2,220	11,200	1,500	16,520

4 Reapportionment of production service cost centre costs to production cost centres

Production service cost centres are not directly involved in making products and therefore the production overheads of service cost centres must be shared out between the production cost centres using a suitable basis. This is known as reapportionment or secondary apportionment.

There are 3 methods that can be used:

- **Direct** method – the cost of each production service cost centre is reapportioned to the production cost centres only.
- **Step down** method – used when one production service cost centre works or provides a service for other production service cost centres as well as the production cost centres.
- **Reciprocal** reapportionment (or the repeated distribution method) – used where production service cost centres work for each other as well as provide a service for the production cost centres.

Illustration 2 – Direct reapportionment

The total overheads allocated and apportioned to the production and service cost centres of LS Ltd are as follows:

Assembly	= $17,350
Finishing	= $23,970
Maintenance	= $18,600
Canteen	= $6,600

The canteen feeds the staff that work for the company in Assembly and Finishing. The number of employees in each cost centre:

	Assembly	Finishing	Maintenance	Canteen
Number of employees	18	30	12	2

The amount of time spent by the maintenance cost centre servicing equipment in the Assembly and Finishing cost centres has been analysed as follows:

Assembly	60%
Finishing	40%

Required:

Complete the overhead analysis sheet.

Solution

(W1) Canteen overheads are reapportioned on the basis of number of employees that work in the cost centres it services.

Total employees that eat in the canteen = 18 + 30 = 48

Reapportioned to Assembly cost centre = 18/48 × $6,600 = $2,475

Reapportioned to Finishing cost centre = 30/48 × $6,600 = $4,125

(W2) Assembly = 60% × $18,600 = $11,160

Finishing = 40% × $18,600 = $7,440

Overhead	*Basis of apportionment*	*Assembly $*	*Finishing $*	*Maintenance $*	*Canteen $*	*Total $*
Total from above		17,350	23,970	18,600	6,600	66,520
Reapportion canteen	Employees (W1)	2,475	4,125	–	(6,600)	–
Reapportion maintenance	% time (W2)	11,160	7,440	(18,600)	–	–
Total		30,985	35,535	0	0	66,520

Illustration 3 – Step down reapportionment

The total overheads allocated and apportioned to the production and service cost centres of LS Ltd are as follows:

Assembly	= $17,350
Finishing	= $23,970
Maintenance	= $18,600
Canteen	= $6,600

The canteen feeds all the staff that work for the company in maintenance, finishing and assembly but the maintenance staff do not provide support for the canteen equipment.

The amount of time spent by the maintenance cost centre servicing equipment in the Assembly and Finishing cost centres has been analysed as follows:

Assembly	60%
Finishing	40%

The number of employees in each cost centre:

	Assembly	Finishing	Maintenance	Canteen
Number of employees	18	30	12	2

Required:

Complete the overhead analysis sheet.

Solution

Workings

(W1) Canteen overheads are reapportioned on the basis of the number of employees that work in the cost centres it serves

Total employees that eat in the canteen = 18 + 30 + 12 = 60

Reapportioned to Assembly department = 18/60 × $6,600 = $1,980

(W2) Assembly = 60% × $19,920 = $11,952

Finishing = 40% × $19,920 = $7,968

Overhead	*Basis of apportionment*	*Assembly* $	*Finishing* $	*Maintenance* $	*Canteen* $	*Total* $
Total from above		17,350	23,970	18,600	6,600	66,520
Reapportion canteen	Employees (W1)	1,980	3,300	1,320	(6,600)	–
Subtotal		19,330	27,270	19,920	0	66,520
Reapportion maintenance	% time (W2)	11,952	7,968	(19,920)	–	–
Total		31,282	35,238	0	0	66,520

Test your understanding 1

A manufacturing company runs two production cost centres C1 and C2, and two service cost centres S1 and S2. The total allocated and apportioned overheads for each is as follows:

C1	**C2**	**S1**	**S2**
$12,000	$17,000	$9,500	$8,000

It has been estimated that each service cost centre does work for other cost centres in the following proportions:

	C1	**C2**	**S1**	**S2**
Percentage of service cost centre S1 to:	60%	40%	–	–
Percentage of service cost centre S2 to:	35%	35%	30%	–

After the reapportionment of service cost centre costs has been carried out, what is the total overhead for production cost centre C1?

A $17,700

B $19,140

C $21,940

D $23,240

Illustration 4 – Reciprocal reapportionment

The total overheads allocated and apportioned to the production and service cost centres of LS Ltd are as follows.

Assembly	= $17,350
Finishing	= $23,970
Maintenance	= $18,600
Canteen	= $6,600

The maintenance costs are to be reapportioned on the basis of time spent servicing equipment:

	Assembly	Finishing	Maintenance	Canteen
Time spent	50%	40%	–	10%

The Canteen cost centre's overheads are to be reapportioned on the basis of the number of employees in the other three cost centres.

	Assembly	Finishing	Maintenance	Canteen
Number of employees	18	30	12	2

Required:

Complete the overhead analysis sheet below and reapportion the service cost centres' overheads to the production cost centres.

Solution

(W1) reapportioned canteen to assembly = 18/60 × 6,600 = 1,980

(W2) reapportioned maintenance to assembly = 50% × 19,920 = 9,960

(W3) reapportioned canteen to assembly = 18/60 × 1,992 = 598

(W4) reapportioned maintenance to assembly = 50% × 398 = 199

Overhead	*Assembly* *$*	*Finishing* *$*	*Maintenance* *$*	*Canteen* *$*	*Total* *$*
Total from above	17,350	23,970	18,600	6,600	66,520
Reapportion canteen **(W1)**	1,980	3,300	1,320	(6,600)	–
Reapportion maintenance **(W2)**	9,960	7,968	(19,920)	1,992	–
Reapportion canteen **(W3)**	598	996	398	(1,992)	–
Reapportion maintenance **(W4)**	199	159	(398)	40	–
Reapportion canteen	12	20	8	(40)	–
Reapportion maintenance	4	3	(8)	1	–
Reapportion canteen	0	1	–	(1)	–
Total	30,103	36,417	0	0	66,520

Solution – Using equations

There is another option for calculating the total overhead in each production cost centre. Some people will find it a quicker option but others prefer to reapportion as in the previous solution. Whichever you choose you should arrive at the same answer.

Often you will find that the data for reapportioning is given in percentages. The amount of time spent by the maintenance cost centre servicing equipment in the other three cost centres has been analysed as percentages.

Assembly 50%
Finishing 40%
Canteen 10%

In this illustration we need to convert the relevant number of employees into percentages.

	Assembly	Finishing	Maintenance
Number of employees	18	30	12
Number of employees as a %	18/60 × 100 = 30%	30/60 × 100 = 50%	12/60 × 100 = 20%

Now we can produce two calculations that show the relationship between Maintenance and Canteen – the two service cost centres.

Maintenance = $18,600 (overhead already apportioned) + 20% of the Canteen overhead

Canteen = $6,600 (overhead already apportioned) + 10% of the Maintenance overhead

These can be shortened to:

M = 18,600 + 20%C

C = 6,600 + 10%M

Currently each formula has 2 unknowns in them – M and C. We can substitute one of the formulae into the other to calculate the unknowns:

M = 18,600 + 20%(6,600 + 10%M)

M is the only unknown.

Change the % to decimals.

M = 18,600 + 0.2(6,600 + 0.1 M)

Remove the brackets.

M = 18,600 + (0.2 × 6,600) + (0.2 × 0.1 M)

M = 18,600 + 1,320 + 0.02M

Put the 'unknowns' together.

M – 0.02M = 18,600 + 1,320 0.98M = 19,920

Therefore **M = 19,920/0.98 = $20,327**

We now know M so can substitute into the formula for C.

C = 6,600 + 10%M

C = 6,600 + 0.1 × 20,327

C = $8,633

Final step is to then relate these amounts to the production centres:

Assembly = 17,350 + 0.5M + 0.3C

Assembly = 17,350 + (0.5 × 20,327) + (0.3 × 8,633)

Assembly = $30,103

Finishing = 23,970 + 0.4M + 0.5C

Finishing = 23,970 + (0.4 × 20,327) + (0.5 × 8,633)

Finishing = $36,417

Test your understanding 2

A company has three production cost centres, Alpha, Beta and Gamma, and two service cost centres, Maintenance (M) and Payroll (P). The following table shows how costs have been allocated and the relative usage of each service cost centre by other cost centres.

	Production			**Service**	
Cost centre	**Alpha**	**Beta**	**Gamma**	**M**	**P**
Costs	$3,000	$4,000	$2,000	$2,500	$2,700
Proportion M (%)	20	30	25	–	25
Proportion P (%)	25	25	30	20	–

Required:

Complete the overhead analysis sheet below and reapportion the service cost centre overheads to the production cost centres using the reciprocal method.

Overhead	Alpha $	Beta $	Gamma $	M $	P $
Total overheads					
Reapportion M					
Reapportion P					
Reapportion M					
Reapportion P					
Reapportion M					
Reapportion P					
Total					

5 Absorption of overheads

Bases of absorption

Once the overheads are allocated, apportioned and reapportioned into the production cost centres the overheads need to be related to or absorbed into the units of product.

- Overheads can also be absorbed into cost units using the following absorption bases:
  - units produced
  - machine-hour rate (when production is machine intensive)
  - labour-hour rate (when production is labour intensive)
  - percentage of prime cost
  - percentage of direct wages.
- Production overheads are usually calculated at the beginning of an accounting period in order to determine how much cost to assign to a unit before calculating a selling price.

- The overhead absorption rate (OAR) is calculated as follows:

$$\text{OAR} = \frac{\textbf{Budgeted production overhead}}{\textbf{Budgeted total of absorption basis}}$$

- The absorption basis is most commonly units of a product, labour hours, or machine hours.

It is usual for a product to pass through more than one cost centre during the production process. Each cost centre will normally have a separate OAR.

- For example, a machining cost centre will probably use a machine-hour OAR.
- Similarly, a labour-intensive cost centre will probably use a labour-hour OAR.

An alternative to individual cost centre OAR is a blanket OAR. With blanket OARs, only one absorption rate is calculated for the entire factory regardless of the cost centres involved in production. Blanket OARs are also known as single factory-wide OARs.

e.g

Illustration 5 – OAR per unit

RS Ltd is a manufacturing company producing Product P, which has the following cost card.

		$
Direct labour	2 hrs @ $5 per hour	10
Direct materials	1 kg @ $5 per kg	5
Direct expenses		1
Prime cost		**16**

RS Ltd produces and sells 1,000 units in a month. RS absorbed overheads based on the number of units produced.

Based on past experience, RS Ltd estimates its monthly overheads will be as follows.

	$
Heating	3,000
Power	2,000
Maintenance	500
Total	5,500

Required

Calculate the total cost of one unit of product P

Solution

	$
Prime cost	16.00
Overheads $5,500/1,000 units	5.50
Total	**21.50**

Illustration 6 – OAR per hour

Ballard Ltd makes three products A, B and C. Each passes through two cost centres: Machining and Assembly.

Budgeted production in each cost centre by each product

	Units	Machining	Assembly
Product A	1,000	1 hr	1 hr
Product B	2,000	2 hrs	1/2 hr
Product C	500	None	4 hrs

Overheads are budgeted as follows:

Machining	Assembly
$100,000	$150,000

Required

(a) Calculate the OAR per hour for each cost centre and the overall blanket OAR per hour.

(b) Calculate the overhead absorbed by Product B based on the individual cost centre OAR per hour

Solution

(a) **Machining**

Total hours = (1,000 × 1) + (2,000 × 2) = 5,000 hours

OAR = $100,000/5,000 hours = $20 per hour

Assembly

Total hours = (1,000 × 1) + (2,000 × 0.5) + (500 × 4) = 4,000 hours

OAR = $150,000/4,000 hours = $37.50

Blanket OAR = $250,000/9,000 hours = 27.78

(b) Overhead absorbed by Product B

= (2 hours × $20) + (0.5 hours × $37.50) = $58.75

Test your understanding 3

The Major Gnome Manufacturing Company has two cost centres – Moulding and Painting – and uses a single production OAR based on direct labour hours. The budget and actual data for Period 6 are given below:

	Direct wages $	Labour hours	Machine hours	Production overhead $
Budget				
Moulding	24,000	4,000	12,000	180,000
Painting	70,000	10,000	1,000	100,000
	94,000	14,000	13,000	280,000
Actual				
Moulding	30,000	5,000	14,000	200,000
Painting	59,500	8,500	800	95,000
	89,500	13,500	4,800	295,000

During Period 6, a batch of Pixie Gnomes was made, with the following costs and times:

	Direct wages $	Labour hours	Machine hours
Moulding	726	120	460
Painting	2,490	415	38
	3,216	535	498

The direct material cost of the batch was $890.

Complete the following.

(a) Using a single blanket OAR based on labour hours:

The cost of the batch of Pixie Gnomes is $

(b) It has been suggested that appropriate cost centre OARs may be more realistic. The OAR in:

(i) the moulding cost centre is $

(ii) the painting cost centre is $

(c) Using cost centre OARs:

The cost of the batch of Pixie Gnomes is $

6 Under- and over-absorption of overheads

If the estimates for the budgeted overheads and/or the budgeted level of activity are different from the actual results for the year then this will lead to one of the following:

- under-absorption (recovery) of overheads
- over-absorption (recovery) of overheads.

Calculating an under- or over-absorption

There is a three step procedure:

Step 1 – calculate the OAR (based on budget)

$$\textbf{OAR} = \frac{\textbf{Budgeted overheads}}{\textbf{Budgeted level of activity}}$$

Step 2 – calculate the overhead absorbed by actual activity

Overheads absorbed = OAR × actual level of activity

Step 3 – Compare absorbed to actual

If at the end of this period, the overheads **absorbed are greater than the actual** overheads, then there has been an **over-absorption** of overheads.

If the overheads **absorbed are less than the actual** overheads, then there has been an **under-absorption** of overheads.

Illustration 7 – Under- and over-absorption of overheads

The following data relate to Lola Ltd for Period 8.

	Budget	Actual
Overheads	$80,000	$90,000
Labour hours worked	20,000	22,000

Required

Calculate the under or over absorption of overheads

Solution

$$\text{OAR} = \frac{\$80,000}{20,000} = \$4 \text{ per labour hour worked}$$

Overhead absorbed = 22,000 × $4 = $88,000

Actual overhead = $90,000

Under-absorbed overhead = $2,000

Test your understanding 4

The following data relate to Lola Ltd for Period 9.

	Budget	**Actual**
Overheads	$148,750	$146,200
Machine hours	8,500	7,928

Overheads were under/over* absorbed by $

* delete as appropriate

Working backwards

Sometimes you may be given information relating to the actual under- or over-absorption in a period and be expected to calculate the budgeted overheads or the actual number of hours worked.

Approach to working backwards

- As long as you remember the basic calculation involved in identifying an under/over-absorption, you should not have any problems.
- The main thing to remember is that if actual overheads are greater than absorbed overheads then we have under-absorption and any under-absorption need to be deducted from actual overheads incurred in order to calculate the overheads absorbed.
- Similarly, if over-absorption occurs, the over-absorption needs to be added to actual overhead in order to calculate the overheads absorbed.

Illustration 8 – Under- and over-absorption of overheads

A business absorbs its fixed production overhead on the basis of direct labour hours. The budgeted direct labour hours for week 24 were 4,200. During that week 4,050 direct labour hours were worked and the production overhead incurred was $16,700. The overhead was under-absorbed by $1,310.

Required:

Calculate the budgeted fixed overhead for the week (to the nearest $10)

Solution

Actual overhead	$16,700
Under-absorbed	$(1,310)
Overhead absorbed	$15,390

$$\text{OAR} = \frac{15{,}390}{4{,}050} = \$3.80 \text{ per hour}$$

Budgeted fixed overhead = 4,200 × $3.80 = $15,960

Test your understanding 5

A business absorbs its fixed overheads on the basis of machine hours worked. The following figures are available for the month of June:

Budgeted fixed overhead	$45,000
Budgeted machine hours	30,000
Actual fixed overhead	$49,000

If there was an over-absorption of overhead of $3,500, how many machine hours were worked in the month?

A 30,334

B 32,667

C 35,000

D 49,000

Diagrams of under- and over- absorption

If we consider that the budgeted overhead cost is fixed (it is budgeted to be a set amount) and the actual overhead cost is also a fixed amount (it has actually been incurred and is not going to change), then we could also assume that the overhead that is being absorbed behaves like a variable cost – the more actual activity there is the more cost will be absorbed.

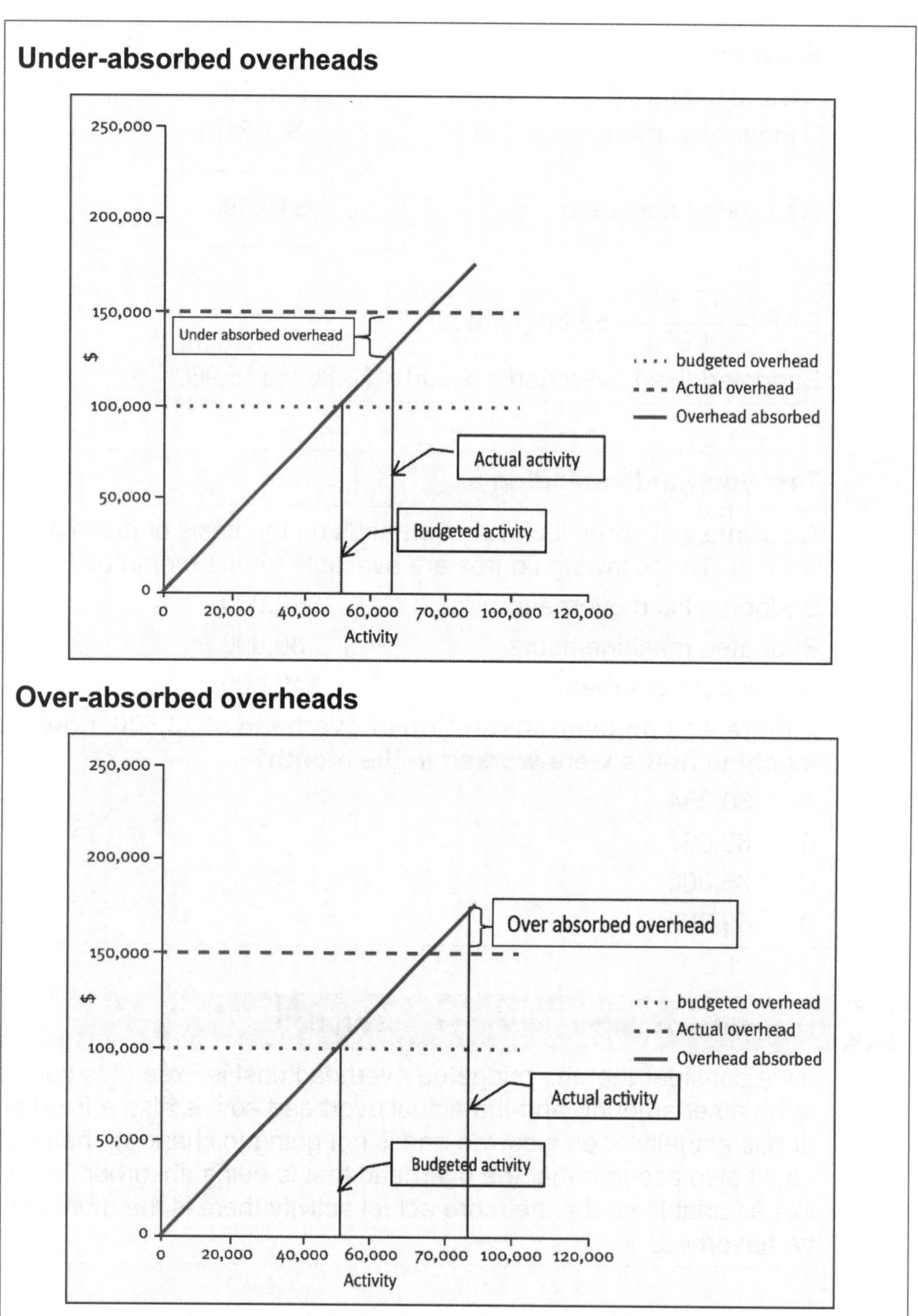
Under-absorbed overheads
250,000
200,000
150,000
100,000
50,000
0
$
Under absorbed overhead
Actual activity
Budgeted activity
budgeted overhead
Actual overhead
Overhead absorbed
0
20,000
40,000
60,000
70,000
100,000
120,000
Activity
Over-absorbed overheads
250,000
200,000
150,000
100,000
50,000
0
$
Over absorbed overhead
Actual activity
Budgeted activity
budgeted overhead
Actual overhead
Overhead absorbed
0
20,000
40,000
60,000
70,000
100,000
120,000
Activity

7 Accounting for production overheads

Production overheads account

Illustration 9 – Journal and ledger entries for manufacturing

Production overheads

	$000		$000
Indirect Labour (1)	20	WIP (2)	108
Indirect Expenses (1)	92	Under-absorption (Bal. figure) (3)	9
Indirect Material (1)	5		
	117		117

Over/under-absorption of overheads

	$000		$000
Production overheads (3)	9	Statement of profit or loss	9
	9		9

1 The production overheads account acts as a collecting place for all the indirect costs of a production process. All the costs are debited to this account.

2 Production overheads are absorbed into production on the basis of actual activity. The absorbed overheads are 'credited out' of the production overheads account and transferred to the WIP account where they are added to the cost of production, and hence the cost of sales.

3 The difference between the overheads absorbed and the overheads actually incurred is either a under- or over-absorption. This is the balancing figure and is transferred to the Over/under-absorption of overheads account. A debit balancing amount in the production overheads accounts is an over-absorption and a credit balancing amount is an under-absorption.

4 At the end of an accounting period, the balance on the over/under-absorption account is transferred to the statement of profit or loss where it is written off (under-absorbed overhead) or increases profit (over-absorbed overhead).

Test your understanding 6

Transaction	Debit which account?	Credit which account?
Indirect materials issued from stores		
Indirect wages analysed in the labour account		
Indirect expenses purchased (cash)		
Production overheads absorbed into the cost of production		
Direct materials issued from stores		

8 Chapter summary

Recap of direct and indirect expenses

- **Direct expenses are part of the prime cost of a product**
- **Indirect expenses are known as overheads**

Journal and ledger entries for manufacturing overheads

Accounting for overheads

Relating non-production overheads to cost units

Allocation and apportionment

- Allocation charges overheads directly to specific departments
- If overheads relate to more than one specific department they must be apportioned (shared) between departments
- Apportioned fixed production overheads include: rent, rates, heating and electricity costs

Reapportionment of service cost centre costs to production cost centres

Reapportionment involves sharing out the fixed production overheads of service cost centres between production cost centres

Basic method – one service department does work for another, but not vice versa

Production overhead absorption

Reciprocal method – both service departments do work for each other

Appropriate bases for absorption

- Machine-hour rate
- Labour-hour rate
- Percentage of prime cost
- Percentage of direct wages

Under- and over-absorption of overheads

If either or both of the estimates for budgeted overheads or budgeted level of activity are different from actual results then this will lead to under-or-over-absorption (recovery) of overheads

Test your understanding answers

Test your understanding 1

C

Allocated and apportioned overheads $12,000

Add: reapportionment of S1: 60% × $9,500 = $5,700

Add: reapportionment of S2 overhead apportioned to S1: $8000 × 30% × 60% = $1,440

Add: reapportionment of S2: 35% × $8,000 = $2,800

Total = $21,940

Test your understanding 2

Overhead	Alpha $	Beta $	Gamma $	M $	P $
Total overheads	3,000	4,000	2,000	2,500	2,700
Reapportion M	500	750	625	(2,500)	625
	(20%)	(30%)	(25%)		(25%)
Reapportion P	831	831	998	665	(3,325)
	(25%)	(25%)	(30%)	(20%)	
Reapportion M	133	200	166	(665)	166
	(20%)	(30%)	(25%)		(25%)
Reapportion P	41	42	50	33	(166)
	(25%)	(25%)	(30%)	(20%)	
Reapportion M	7	10	8	(33)	8
	(20%)	(30%)	(25%)		(25%)
Reapportion P	3	2	3		(8)
	(25%)	(25%)	(30%)		
Total	4,515	5,835	3,850		

Alternative answer (using equations)

M = 2,500 + 20% P

and

P = 2,700 + 25% M

Substitute the equation for P into the equation for M to have one unknown:

M = 2,500 + 20% (2,700 + 25% M)

Turn the percentages to decimals and multiply out the brackets:

M = 2,500 + (0.2 × 2,700) + (0.2 × 0.25M)
M = 2,500 + 540 + 0.05M

Put the unknowns together:

M – 0.05M = 2,500 + 540
0.95M = 3,040

Calculate was M equals:

M = 3,040/0.95
M = 3,200

Go to original equations to calculate P:

P = 2,700 + 25% M
P = 2,700 + 0.25 × 3,200
P = 3,500

Using the percentages in the original data for Alpha, Beta and Gamma we can calculate how much overhead each cost centre receives:

Alpha = 3,000 + (20% × 3,200) + (25% × 3,500)
Alpha = $4,515

Beta = 4,000 + (30% × 3,200) + (25% × 3,500)
Beta = $5,835

Gamma = 2,000 + (25% × 3,200) + (30% × 3,500)
Gamma = $3,850

Test your understanding 3

(a) Using a single blanket OAR based on labour hours:

The cost of the batch of Pixie Gnomes is **$14,806**

(b) It has been suggested that appropriate cost centre OARs may be more realistic. The OAR in:

(i) the moulding cost centre is **$15**

(ii) the painting cost centre is **$10**

(c) Using cost centre OARs:

The cost of the batch of Pixie Gnomes is **$15,156**

Workings:

$$\text{Blanket OAR} = \frac{\$280,000}{14,000} = \$20 \text{ per labour hour}$$

(a) Cost of batch of Pixie Gnomes

	$
Direct materials	890
Direct labour	3,216
Overheads (535 hours @ $20 per hour)	10,700
TOTAL COST	14,806

(b)

	(i) **Moulding**	(ii) **Painting**
Budgeted overheads	$180,000	$100,000
Budgeted hours	12,000 machine hours	10,000 labour hours
OAR	$15 per machine hour	$10 per labour hour

(c) Cost of a batch of Pixie Gnomes using separate cost centre OARs

	$
Direct materials	890
Direct labour	3,216
Moulding overheads (460 × $15)	6,900
Painting overheads (415 × $10)	4,150
TOTAL COST	15,156

Test your understanding 4

Overheads were under absorbed by		$7,460

OAR =	$\frac{\$148,750}{8,500}$	= $17.50 per machine hour
Overhead absorbed		= 7,928 × $17.50 = $138,740
Actual overhead		= $146,200
Under-absorbed overhead		= $7,460

Test your understanding 5

C

35,000 machine hours were worked in the month.

Workings:

OAR =	$\frac{\$45,000}{30,000}$	= $1.50 per hour
Actual overhead	$49,000	
Over-absorbed overhead	$3,500	
Absorbed overhead	$52,500	

$$\text{Machine hours worked} = \frac{\text{Overheads absorbed}}{\text{Overhead absorption rate}}$$

$$= \frac{\$52,500}{\$1.50}$$

$$= 35,000 \text{ hours}$$

Test your understanding 6

Transaction	Debit which account?	Credit which account?
Indirect materials issued from stores	Production overheads account	Material inventory account
Indirect wages analysed in the labour account	Production overheads account	Labour account
Indirect expenses purchased (cash)	Production overheads account	Bank
Production overheads absorbed into the cost of production	WIP account	Production overheads account
Direct materials issued from stores	WIP account	Material inventory account

Chapter

6

Absorption and marginal costing

Chapter learning objectives

Upon completion of this chapter you will be able to:

- explain the importance of, and apply, the concept of contribution
- demonstrate and discuss the effect of absorption and marginal costing on inventory valuation and profit determination
- calculate profit or loss under absorption and marginal costing
- reconcile the profits or losses calculated under absorption and marginal costing
- describe the advantages and disadvantages of absorption and marginal costing.

One of the PER performance objectives (PO12) is to apply different management accounting techniques is different business contexts to effectively manage and use resources. Working through this chapter should help you understand how to demonstrate that objective.

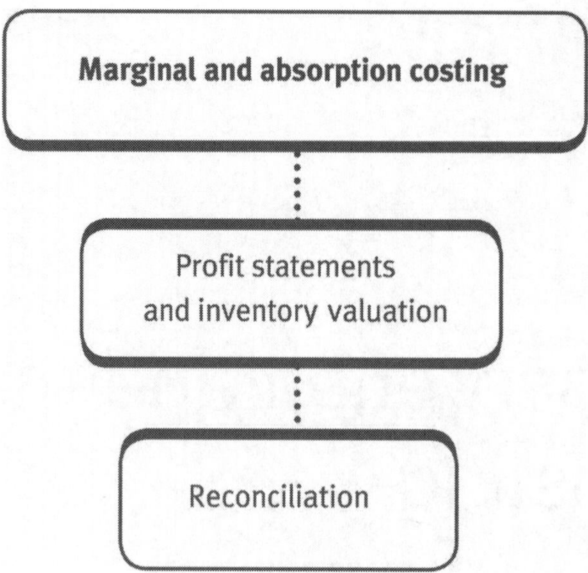

1 Introduction

Marginal and absorption costing are two different ways of valuing the cost of units sold and finished units in inventory. The basic unit cost consists of the direct costs; the difference arises due to the treatment of the production overheads:

- absorption costing assigns both the fixed and variable production overheads to each unit. See Chapter 5 for the allocation, apportionment, reapportionment and absorption techniques.
- marginal costing only assigns variable productions overheads to each unit. Fixed production overheads are treated as period costs.

2 Marginal costing

The marginal production cost is the cost of one unit of product or service which would be avoided if that unit were not produced, or which would increase if one extra unit were produced.

The **marginal** cost of a unit of inventory is the total of the **variable** costs required to produce the unit (the marginal cost). This includes direct materials, direct labour, direct expenses and variable production overheads.

No fixed overheads are included in the inventory valuation; they are treated as a period cost and deducted in full against the profits for the period.

Marginal costing is the principal costing technique used in decision making. The key reason for this is that the marginal costing approach allows management's attention to be focused on the changes which result from the decision under consideration.

The contribution concept

The contribution concept lies at the heart of marginal costing. Contribution can be calculated as follows:

Contribution = Sales price – All variable costs

Illustration 1 – The concept of contribution

The following information relates to a company that makes a single product – a desk lamp.

	Per lamp		Sales of 1,000 lamps		Sales of 1,500 lamps
	$	$	$	$	$
Sales revenue	600		600,000		900,000
Direct materials	200	200,000		300,000	
Direct labour	150	150,000		225,000	
Variable production overheads	50	50,000		75,000	
Marginal cost of production			**(400,000)**		**(600,000)**
Contribution			**200,000**		**300,000**
Fixed production overheads			(120,000)		(120,000)
Total profit			80,000		180,000
Contribution per lamp			**200**		**200**
Profit per lamp			80		120

Fixed costs have been estimated to be $120,000 based on a production level of 1,000 lamps and it expected to remain at this level.

- Profit per lamp has increased from $80 when 1,000 lamps are sold to $120 when 1,500 lamps are sold.
- Contribution per lamp has remained constant at both levels of sales.

Using profit per unit is not particularly useful when making short term decisions as profit per unit depends on how many units are sold. For this reason, the contribution concept is frequently employed by management accountants.

- Contribution gives an idea of how much 'money' there is available to 'contribute' towards paying for the fixed costs of the organisation.
- At varying levels of output and sales, contribution per unit is constant.
- Contribution per unit = Sales price per unit – total variable cost per unit
- Total contribution = Contribution per unit × Sales volume.
- Profit = Total contribution – Fixed overheads.

Test your understanding 1

Buhner Ltd makes only one product, the cost card of which is:

	$
Direct materials	3
Direct labour	6
Variable production overhead	2
Fixed production overhead	4
Variable selling cost	5

The selling price of one unit is $25.

Budgeted fixed overheads are based on budgeted production of 5,000 units.

Sales during the period were 3,000 units and actual fixed production overheads incurred were $25,000.

(a) Calculate the total contribution earned during the period.

(b) Calculate the total profit or loss for the period.

3 Absorption costing

Absorption costing is a method of building up a full product cost which adds direct costs and a proportion of production overhead costs by means of one or a number of overhead absorption rates.

Absorption costing values each unit of inventory at the cost incurred to **produce** the unit. This includes an amount added to the cost of each unit to represent the **production** overheads incurred by that product. The amount added to each unit is based on estimates made at the start of the period.

To calculate a production cost per unit the budgeted production costs are divided by the budgeted activity. The calculation of the cost per unit (overhead absorption rate) was looked at in more detail in Chapter 5 – Accounting for overheads.

4 Inventory valuation and profit determination

Absorption and marginal costing

Marginal costing values inventory at the variable production cost of a unit of product.

Absorption costing values inventory at the full production cost of a unit of product.

- Inventory values will therefore be different at the beginning and end of a period under marginal and absorption costing.
- If inventory values are different, this will have an effect on profits reported in the statement of profit or loss in a period.
- Profits determined using marginal costing principles will therefore be different to those using absorption costing principles.

Absorption costing statement of profit or loss

In order to be able to prepare a statement of profit or loss under absorption costing, you need to be able to complete the following proforma:

Absorption costing statement of profit or loss

	$	$
Sales		X
Less: Cost of sales:		
Opening inventory	X	
Variable cost of production	X	
Fixed overhead absorbed	X	
Less closing inventory	(X)	
		(X)
		X
(under)/over-absorption		(X)/X
Gross profit		X
Less Non-production costs		(X)
Profit/loss		X

- **Valuation of inventory** – opening and closing inventory are valued at full production cost under absorption costing.
- **Under/over-absorbed overhead** – an adjustment for under or over absorption of overheads is necessary in absorption costing statements.
- Absorption costing statements are split into **production** costs in the cost of sales and **non-production** costs after gross profit.

Marginal costing statement of profit or loss

In order to be able to prepare a statement of profit or loss under marginal costing, you need to be able to complete the following proforma:

Marginal costing statement of profit or loss

	$	$
Sales		X
Less Cost of sales:		
Opening inventory	X	
Variable cost of production	X	
Less closing inventory	(X)	
		(X)
		X
Less Other variable costs		(X)
Contribution		X
Less fixed costs		(X)
Profit/loss		X

- **Valuation of inventory** – opening and closing inventory are valued at marginal (variable) cost under marginal costing.
- The fixed costs **incurred** are deducted from contribution earned in order to determine the profit for the period.
- Marginal costing statements are split into all the variable costs before contribution and all the fixed costs after contribution.
- **Note:** only the production variable costs are included in the cost of sales and valuation of inventory. If there are variable non-production costs (i.e. selling costs) these would be deducted before contribution but not included in the cost of sales.

Illustration 2 – Impact of inventory on profit

A company commenced business on 1 March making one product only, the cost card of which is as follows:

	$
Direct labour	5
Direct material	8
Variable production overhead	2
Fixed production overhead	5
Standard production cost	20

The fixed production overhead figure has been calculated on the basis of a budgeted normal output of 36,000 units per annum. The fixed production overhead actually incurred in March was $15,000.

Selling, distribution and administration expenses are:

Fixed	$10,000 per month
Variable	15% of the sales value

The selling price per unit is $50 and the number of units produced and sold were:

Production	2,000
Sales	1,500

Prepare the absorption costing and marginal costing statements of profit or loss for March.

Absorption costing statement of profit or loss – March

	$	$
Sales		75,000
Less Cost of sales: (full production cost)		
Opening inventory	–	
Variable cost of production (2,000 × $15)	30,000	
Fixed production overhead absorbed (2,000 × $5)	10,000	
Less Closing inventory **(W1)** (500 × $20)	(10,000)	
		(30,000)
(Under)/over-absorption **(W2)**		(5,000)
Gross profit		40,000
Less Non-production costs **(W3)**		(21,250)
Profit/loss		18,750

Workings

(W1) Closing inventory = opening inventory + production – sales units
= 0 + 2,000 – 1,500 = 500 units

(W2)

	$
Overheads absorbed (2,000 × $5)	10,000
Overheads incurred	15,000
Under-absorption on overheads	5,000

(W3)

Fixed = 10,000

Variable = 15% × $75,000 = $11,250

Total = $(10,000 + 11,250) = $21,250

Marginal costing statement of profit or loss – March

	$	$
Sales		75,000
Less Cost of sales: (marginal production costs)		
Opening inventory	–	
Variable cost of production (2,000 × $15)	30,000	
Less Closing inventory (500 × $15)	(7,500)	
		(22,500)
		52,500
Less Other variable costs (15% × $75,000)		(11,250)
Contribution		41,250
Less Total fixed costs (actually incurred) $(15,000 + 10,000)		(25,000)
Profit/loss		16,250

Test your understanding 2

Duo Ltd makes and sells one product, the Alpha. The following information is available for period 3:

Production (units)	2,500
Sales (units)	2,300
Opening inventory (units)	0

Financial data:	*Alpha*
	$
Unit selling price	90
Unit cost:	
direct materials	15
direct labour	18
variable production overheads	12
fixed production overheads	30
variable selling overheads	1

Fixed production overheads for the period were $52,500 and fixed administration overheads were $13,500.

Required:

(a) Prepare a statement of profit or loss for period 3 based on marginal costing principles.

(b) Prepare a statement of profit or loss for period 3 based on absorption costing principles.

Reconciling profits reported under the different methods

When inventory levels increase or decrease during a period then profits differ under absorption and marginal costing.

- If inventory levels increase, absorption costing gives the higher profit.
- If inventory levels decrease, marginal costing gives the higher profit.
- If inventory levels are constant, both methods give the same profit.

Illustration 3 – Reconciling profits

A company commenced business on 1 March making one product only, the cost card of which is as follows (details as per illustration 2).

	$
Direct labour	5
Direct material	8
Variable production overhead	2
Fixed production overhead	5
Full production cost	20

- Marginal cost of production = 5 + 8 + 2 = $15
- Absorption cost of production = 5 + 8 + 2 + 5 = $20
- Difference in cost of production = $5 which is the fixed production overhead element of the absorption cost of production.
- This means that each unit of opening and closing inventory will be valued at $5 more under absorption costing.

The number of units produced and sold was as follows.

	March (units)
Production	2,000
Sales	1,500

Closing inventory is 500 units (as calculated in illustration 2)

- Profit for March under absorption costing = $18,750 (as calculated in illustration 2).
- Profit for March under marginal costing = $16,250 (as calculated in illustration 2).
- Difference in profits = $18,750 – $16,250 = $2,500.

This difference can be analysed as follows

Absorption costing:

- There are zero opening inventories so no fixed production costs have been brought forward.
- $10,000 of fixed production costs have been charged to production (2,000 units × $5).
- $2,500 of this has then been deducted from the cost of sales as part of the closing inventory value (500 × $5).
- An adjustment for the under-absorption of $5,000 has been charged.
- Therefore **$12,500** of fixed costs has been charged in this month's statement of profit or loss ($10,000 – $2,500 + $5,000).

Marginal costing:

- The statement of profit or loss is charged with the full **$15,000** of fixed production overhead costs as none are included in the cost of sales.

Reconciliation:

- Inventory levels are increasing by 500 units (zero opening inventory and 500 units of closing inventory)
- $2,500 ($15,000 – $12,500) less cost is charged in the period using absorption costing principles when compared to marginal costing principles therefore the profit will be $2,500 higher under absorption costing principles.

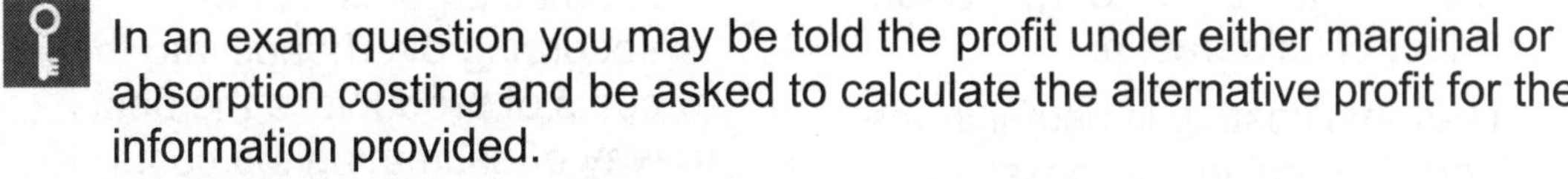

In an exam question you may be told the profit under either marginal or absorption costing and be asked to calculate the alternative profit for the information provided.

There is a short cut to reconciling the profits:

Absorption costing profit		18,750
(Opening inventory – Closing inventory) × OAR	(0 – 500) × 5	– 2,500
Marginal costing profit		16,250

Test your understanding 3

(a) In a period where opening inventory was 5,000 units and closing inventory was 3,000 units, a company had a profit of $92,000 using absorption costing. If the fixed overhead absorption rate was $9 per unit, calculate the profit using marginal costing.

(b) When opening inventory was 8,500 litres and closing inventory was 6,750 litres, a company had a profit of $62,100 using marginal costing. The fixed overhead absorption rate was $3 per litre. Calculate the profit using absorption costing.

5 The advantages and disadvantages of absorption and marginal costing

Advantages of marginal costing	Advantages of absorption costing
• Contribution per unit is constant unlike profit per unit which varies with changes in sales volumes. • There is no under or over absorption of overheads (and hence no adjustment is required in the statement of profit or loss) • Fixed costs are a period cost and are charged in full to the period under consideration. • Marginal costing is useful in the decision-making process. • It is simple to operate.	• Absorption costing includes an element of fixed production overheads in inventory values (in accordance with IAS 2). • Analysing under/over absorption of overheads is a useful exercise in controlling costs of an organisation. • In small organisations, absorbing overheads into the costs of products is the best way of estimating job costs and profits on jobs

- The main disadvantages of marginal costing are that closing inventory is not valued in accordance with IAS 2 principles and that fixed production overheads are not 'shared' out between units of production, but written off in full instead.
- The main disadvantages of absorption costing are that it is more complex to operate than marginal costing and it does not provide as much useful information for short term decision making.

6 Chapter summary

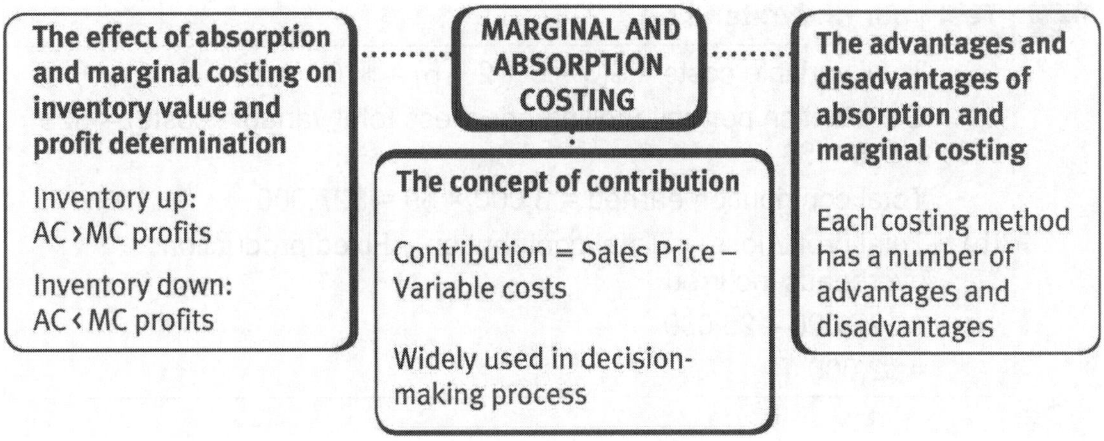

MARGINAL AND ABSORPTION COSTING

The effect of absorption and marginal costing on inventory value and profit determination

Inventory up:
AC > MC profits

Inventory down:
AC < MC profits

The concept of contribution

Contribution = Sales Price – Variable costs

Widely used in decision-making process

The advantages and disadvantages of absorption and marginal costing

Each costing method has a number of advantages and disadvantages

Test your understanding answers

Test your understanding 1

(a) Total variable costs = $(3 + 6 + 2 + 5) = $16

Contribution per unit (selling price less total variable costs) = $25 – $16 = $9

Total contribution earned = 3,000 × $9 = $27,000

(b) Total profit/(loss) = Total contribution – Fixed production overheads incurred

= $27,000 – 25,000

= $2,000

Test your understanding 2

(a) Marginal costing

	$000	$000
Sales		207
Opening inventory	–	
Variable production cost (2,500 × 45)	112.5	
Closing inventory (200 × 45)	(9)	
		(103.5)
		103.5
Variable selling costs (2,300 × $1)		(2.3)
Contribution		101.2
Fixed production costs		(52.5)
Fixed administration costs		(13.5)
Profit		35.2

(b) Absorption costing

	$000	$000
Sales		207
Opening inventory	–	
Full production cost (2,500 × 75)	187.5	
Closing inventory (200 × 75)	(15)	
		(172.5)
		34.5
Over-absorbed overhead (working)		22.5
Gross profit		57
Less: non-production overheads		
variable selling overheads		(2.3)
fixed administration overheads		(13.5)
Profit		41.2

Working

	$
Overhead absorbed = (2,500 × $30)	75,000
Overheads incurred =	52,500
Over-absorbed overhead	22,500

Test your understanding 3

(a)

Absorption costing profit	$92,000
Difference in profit = change in inventory × fixed cost per unit = (5,000 – 3,000) × $9	$18,000
Marginal costing profit	$110,000

Since inventory levels have fallen in the period, marginal costing shows the higher profit figure, therefore marginal costing profit will be $18,000 higher than the absorption costing profit, i.e. $110,000.

(b)

Marginal costing profit	$62,100
Difference in profit = change in inventory × fixed cost per unit = (8,500 – 6,750) × $3	$(5,250)
Absorption costing profit	$56,850

Inventory levels have fallen in the period and therefore marginal costing profits will be higher than absorption costing profits. Absorption costing profit is therefore $5,250 less than the marginal costing profit.

The answer could also be calculated working back up from the marginal costing profit:

Absorption costing profit	$56,850
Difference in profit = change in inventory × fixed cost per unit = (8,500 – 6,750) × $3	$5,250
Marginal costing profit	$62,100

Chapter

7

Job, batch and process costing

Chapter learning objectives

Upon completion of this chapter you will be able to:

- Job and batch costing:
  - describe the characteristics of job and batch costing
  - describe the situation where the use of job or batch costing would be appropriate
  - prepare cost records and accounts in job and batch costing situations
  - establish job and batch costs from given information
- Process costing:
  - describe the characteristics of process costing
  - describe situations where the use of process costing would be appropriate
  - explain the concepts of normal and abnormal losses and abnormal gains
  - calculate the cost per unit of process outputs
  - prepare process accounts involving normal and abnormal losses and abnormal gains
  - calculate and explain the concept of equivalent units
  - apportion process costs between work remaining in process and transfers out of a process using the weighted average and FIFO method (Note: situations involving work-in-progress (WIP) and losses in the same process are excluded)
  - prepare process accounts in situations where work remains incomplete
  - prepare process accounts where losses and gains are identified at different stages of the process
  - distinguish between by-products and joint products

- value by-products and joint products at the point of separation
- prepare process accounts in situations where by-products and/or joint products occur.

One of the PER performance objectives (PO12) is to apply different management accounting techniques is different business contexts to effectively manage and use resources. Working through this chapter should help you understand how to demonstrate that objective.

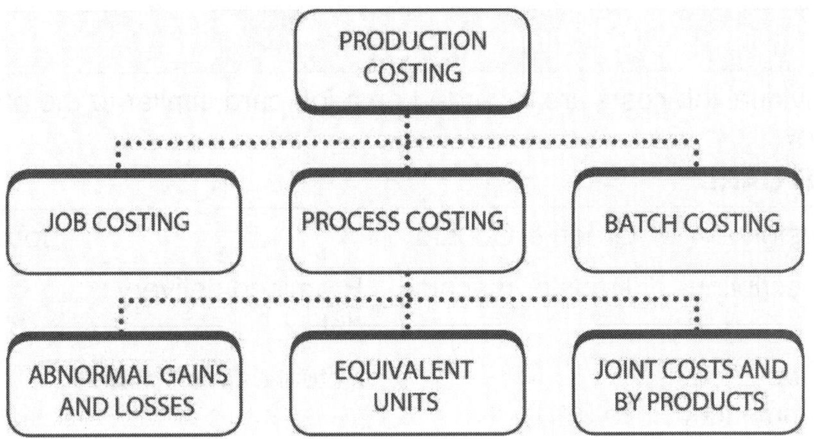

1 Different types of production

Costing systems

- **Specific order costing** is the costing system used when the work done by an organisation consists of **separately identifiable jobs** or **batches**.
- **Continuous operation costing** is the costing method used when goods or services are produced as a direct result of a **sequence of continuous operations or processes**, for example process and service costing.

2 Job and Batch costing

Job costing

Job costing is a form of specific order costing and it is used when a customer orders a specific job to be done. Each job is priced separately and each job is unique.

- The main aim of job costing is to identify the costs associated with completing the order and to record them carefully.
- Individual jobs are given a unique job number and the costs involved in completing the job are recorded on a job cost sheet or job card.
- The selling prices of jobs are calculated by adding a certain amount of profit to the cost of the job.
- Job costing could be used by landscape gardeners where the job would be to landscape a garden; or decorators where the job would be to decorate a room.

Illustration 1 – Job costing

Individual job costs are recorded on a job card similar to the one shown below.

JOB CARD

Customer	Green & Co. Ltd		Job No: 342
Description	Transfer machine	Promised delivery date	3.11.X1
Date commenced	25.9.X1	Actual delivery date	13.11.X1
Price quoted	$2,400		
Despatch note no:	7147		

	Materials estimate $1,250		**Labour estimate $100**		**Overhead estimate $176** Hourly rate $11		**Other charges estimate $25**	
Date Reference	Cost $	Total $	Hrs	Total $	Cost $	Total $	Cost $	Total $
b/f balances		1,200	17	110		187		13
6 Nov Material Requisition 1714	182	1,382						
7 Nov Consultant's test fee							10	23
8 Nov Material Requisition 1937	19	1,401						
9 Nov Material Returns Note	(26)	1,375						
10 Nov Labour analysis			5	138	55	242		

Summary

	$
Materials	1,375
Labour	138
Overhead	242
Other charges	23
	1,778
Invoice price (invoice number 7147 dated 12.12.X1)	2,400
Profit	622

The flow of documents in a job costing system is shown as follows:

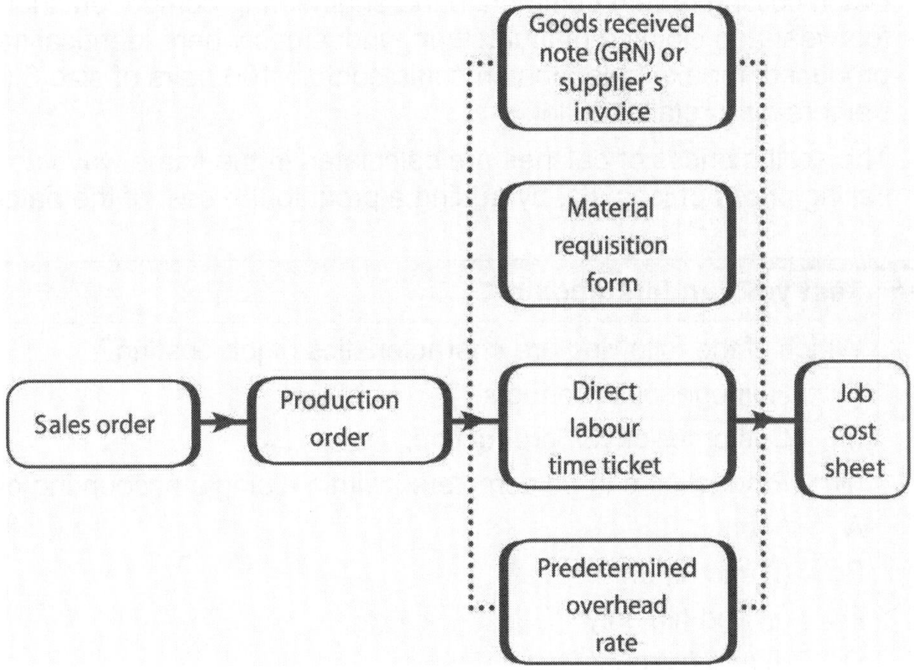

Goods received note (GRN) or supplier's invoice
Material requisition form
Sales order
Production order
Direct labour time ticket
Job cost sheet
Predetermined overhead rate

Batch costing

Batch costing is also a form of specific order costing. It is very similar to job costing.

- Within each batch are a number of identical units but each batch will be different.
- Each batch is a separately identifiable cost unit which is given a batch number in the same way that each job is given a job number.
- Costs can then be collected for each batch number. For example materials requisitions will be coded to a batch number to ensure that the cost of materials used is charged to the correct batch.
- When the batch is completed the unit cost of individual items in the batch is found by dividing the total batch cost by the number of items in the batch.

$$\textbf{Cost per unit in batch} = \frac{\textbf{Total production cost of batch}}{\textbf{Number of units in batch}}$$

- Batch costing is very common in the engineering component industry, footwear and clothing manufacturing industries where identical items are produced; for example a batch could contain 100 pairs of size 6 (UK) trainers for a retailer outlet.
- The selling prices of batches are calculated in the same ways as the selling prices of jobs, i.e. by adding a profit to the cost of the batch.

Test your understanding 1

Which of the following are characteristics of job costing?

(i) Homogenous products.

(ii) Customer-driven production.

(iii) Production can be completed within a single accounting period.

A (i) only

B (i) and (ii) only

C (ii) and (iii) only

D (i) and (iii) only

Illustration 2 – Costing for job and batch costing

Jetprint Ltd specialises in printing advertising leaflets and is in the process of preparing its price list. The most popular requirement is for a folded leaflet made from a single sheet of A4 paper. From past records and budgeted figures, the following data has been estimated for a typical batch of 10,000 leaflets:

Artwork	$65
Machine set up	4 hours @ $22 per hour
Paper	$12.50 per 1,000 sheets
Ink and consumables	$40
Printer's wages 4 hours at	$8 per hour

Note: Printer's wages vary with volume.

General fixed overheads are $15,000 per period during which a total of 600 labour hours are expected to be worked.

Required:

Calculate cost for 10,000 and 20,000 leaflets.

Solution:

	Producing 10,000 leaflets	**Producing 20,000 leaflets**
	$	**$**
Artwork	65	65
Machine set up (4 hours @ $22)	88	88
Paper (variable)	125	250
Ink and consumables (variable)	40	80
Printer's wages ($8 per hour)	32	64
General fixed overheads (W1)	100	200
Total cost	450	747

Workings

Artwork and machine set up are only required once at the start of the production run and are not batch size dependant therefore they are fixed costs.

(W1) Overhead absorption rate = $15,000 ÷ 600 = $25 per hour

For 10,000 leaflets, general fixed overheads = 4 hours × $25 = $100

For 20,000 leaflets, general fixed overheads = 8 hours × $25 = $200

Test your understanding 2

A business has a job costing system and prices jobs using total absorption costing. The cost estimates for Job 264 are as follows:

Direct materials 50 kg @ $4 per kg

Direct labour 30 hours @ $9 per hour

Variable production overhead $6 per direct labour hour

Fixed production overheads are budgeted as $80,000 and are absorbed on the basis of direct labour hours. The total budgeted direct labour hours for the period are 20,000.

Other overheads are recovered at the rate of $40 per job.

Calculate the total job cost for Job 264.

3 Process costing

Process costing is the costing method applicable when goods or services result from a sequence of continuous or repetitive operations or processes. Process costing is used when a company is mass producing the same item and the item goes through a number of different stages.

Process costing is an example of continuous operation costing.

Examples include the chemical, cement, oil refinery, paint and textile industries.

One of the features of process costing is that in most process costing environments the products are identical and indistinguishable from each other. For this reason, an average cost per unit is calculated for each process.

$$\textbf{Average cost per unit} = \frac{\textbf{Net costs of inputs}}{\textbf{Expected output}}$$

- Expected output is what we expect to get out of the process.
- Another feature of process costing is that the output of one process forms the **material** input of the next process.
- When there is closing work-in-progress (WIP) at the end of one period, this forms the opening WIP at the beginning of the next period.

The details of process costs and units are recorded in a process account which shows the materials, labour and overheads input to the process and the materials output at the end of the process.

Illustration 3 – A process account

The following details relate to process 2.

Material transferred from process 1	1,000 units at an average cost of $24 per unit
Labour cost	$9,000
Overhead cost	$3,000
Material transferred to process 3	1,000 units

Required:

Calculate the average cost per unit in Process 2 and complete the Process 2 account.

Solution:

- Balance the units
  Input units = Output units
  1,000 = 1,000
- Calculate the net costs of input
  $24,000 + $9,000 + $3,000 = $36,000
- Calculate the expected output = 1,000 units
- Calculate the average cost per unit = $\frac{\text{Net costs of input}}{\text{Expected output}} = \frac{\$36,000}{1,000} =$ $36
- Value of goods transferred = 1,000 × $36 = $36,000

Process 2 Account

	Units	$		*Units*	$
Transfer from Process 1	1,000	24,000	Transfer to Process 3	1,000	36,000
Direct labour		9,000			
Overheads		3,000			
	1,000	36,000		1,000	36,000

Note that the units completed in Process 1 form the material input into Process 2 and that the units completed in Process 2 form the material input into Process 3.

4 Process costing with losses and gains

Sometimes in a process, the total of the input units may differ from the total of the output units.

- Losses may occur due to the evaporation or wastage of materials and this may be an expected part of the process.
- Losses may sometimes be sold and generate a revenue which is generally referred to as scrap proceeds or scrap value.

Normal loss and scrap value

Normal loss is the loss that is **expected** in a process and it is often expressed as a percentage of the materials input to the process.

- If normal loss is sold as scrap the revenue is used to reduce the input costs of the process. The formula for calculating the average cost of the units output is:

  $$\textbf{Average cost per unit} = \frac{\textbf{Net cost of inputs}}{\textbf{Expected output}}$$

  $$\textbf{Average cost per unit} = \frac{\textbf{Total cost of inputs – Scrap value of normal loss}}{\textbf{Input unit – normal loss units}}$$

- If normal loss has a scrap value, it is valued in the process account at this value.
- If normal loss does not have a scrap value, it is valued in the process account as $Nil.

Illustration 4 – Normal losses

The following data relates to Process 1.

Materials input	1,000 units costing $10,000
Labour costs	$8,000
Overheads	$6,000

Normal loss is 4% of input and is sold as scrap for $12 per unit.

Actual output = 960 units

Required:

Calculate the average cost per unit in Process 1 and produce the process account and the scrap account.

Solution

- Calculate the normal loss units = 4% × 1,000 = 40 units
- Calculate the scrap value of normal loss = 40 units × $12 = $480
- Balance the units (check normal loss is the only loss occurring):
  Input units = Output units + Normal loss
  1,000 = 960 + 40
- Calculate the net cost of inputs
  $10,000 + $8,000 + $6,000 – $480 = $23,520
- Calculate the expected output
  = input units – normal loss units
  = 1,000 units – 40 units = 960 units
- Calculate the average cost per unit
  $\frac{\text{Net costs of input}}{\text{Expected output}} = \frac{\$23,520}{960} = \$24.50$ per unit
- Value of goods transferred = 960 units × $24.50 = $23,520

Process 1 Account

	Units	$		*Units*	$
Materials	1,000	10,000	Transfers to process 2	960	23,520
Labour		8,000	Normal loss	40	480
Overheads		6,000			
	1,000	24,000		1,000	24,000

Scrap Account

	$		$
Process 1 (NL)	480	Cash	480
	480		480

Abnormal losses and gains

Normal loss is the expected loss in a process. If the loss in a process is different to what we are expecting then we have an abnormal loss or an abnormal gain in the process.

 Abnormal loss is more loss than expected

 Abnormal gain is less loss than expected

Abnormal losses and gains and the process account

- The costs associated with producing abnormal losses or gains are not absorbed into the cost of good output.
- Abnormal loss and gain units are valued at the same cost as units of good output in the process account.

Abnormal losses and gains and the scrap account

Losses and gains are transferred from the process account to the abnormal loss/gain account.

If there is no scrap value the losses or gains are transferred to the statement of profit or loss at the value given in the process account.

If there is a scrap value then:

- the abnormal loss is transferred from the abnormal loss/gain account to the scrap account at the scrap value. The cost of the loss transferred to the statement of profit or loss is reduced by the scrap value of these loss units and the cash received for scrap sales is increased by the same amount.
- the abnormal gain is transferred from the abnormal loss/gain account to the scrap account at the scrap value. The saving associated with the gain is transferred to the statement of profit or loss but it also reduces the cash received for the scrap sale.

Illustration 5 – Abnormal losses

The following data relates to Process 1.

Materials input	1,000 units costing $10,000
Labour costs	$8,000
Overheads	$6,000

Normal loss is 4% of input and is sold as scrap for $12 per unit.

Actual output = 944 units

Required:

Calculate the average cost per unit in Process 1 and produce the process account, abnormal gains and losses account and the scrap account.

Solution:

- Calculate the normal loss units = 4% × 1,000 = 40 units
- Calculate the scrap value of normal loss = 40 units × $12 = $480
- Balance the units (identify if there has been extra or less loss)

  Input units = Output units + Normal loss + Abnormal loss

  1,000 = 944 + 40 + 16
- Calculate the net cost of inputs

  $10,000 + $8,000 + $6,000 – $480 = $23,520
- Calculate the expected output

  = input units – normal loss units

  = 1,000 units – 40 units = 960 units
- Calculate the average cost per unit

  $\frac{\text{Net costs of input}}{\text{Expected output}} = \frac{\$23{,}520}{960} = \$24.50$
- Value of goods transferred = 944 × $24.50 = $23,128
- Value the abnormal loss in the process account = 16 × $24.50 = $392

Process 1 Account

	Units	$		*Units*	$
Materials	1,000	10,000	Transfers to process 2	944	23,128
Labour		8,000	Normal loss	40	480
Overheads		6,000	Abnormal loss	16	392
	1,000	24,000		1,000	24,000

- Transfer the abnormal loss to the abnormal loss/gain account at the process account value
- Transfer the normal loss from the process account to the scrap account
- Transfer the abnormal loss from the abnormal loss/gain account at its scrap value = 16 × $12 = $192

Abnormal loss/gain account

	$		$
Process 1 (AL)	392	Scrap	192
		Statement of profit or loss	200
	392		392

Scrap account

	$		$
Process 1 (NL)	480	Cash (56 × $12)	672
Abnormal loss/gain	192		
	672		672

- Balance the abnormal loss/gain account and scrap account
- The balancing figure in the abnormal loss/gain account shows the net loss from having lost more than expected
- The balancing figure in the scrap account represents the cash received for the sale of the loss

Illustration 6 – Abnormal gains

The following data relates to Process 1.

Materials input	1,000 units costing $10,000
Labour costs	$8,000
Overheads	$6,000

Normal loss is 4% of input and is sold as scrap for $12 per unit.

Actual output = 980 units

Required:

Calculate the average cost per unit in Process 1 and produce the process account, abnormal gains and losses account and the scrap account.

Solution:

- Calculate the normal loss units = 4% × 1,000 units = 40 units
- Calculate the scrap value of normal loss = 40 units × $12 = $480
- Balance the units (identify if there has been extra or less loss)

  Input units + Abnormal gain = Output units + Normal loss

  1,000 + 20 = 980 + 40
- Calculate the net cost of inputs

  $10,000 + $8,000 + $6,000 – $480 = $23,520
- Calculate the expected output

  = input units – normal loss units

  = 1,000 units – 40 units = 960 units
- Calculate the average cost per unit

  $\frac{\text{Net costs of input}}{\text{Expected output}} = \frac{\$23{,}520}{960} = \$24.50$
- Value of goods transferred = 980 × $24.50 = $24,010
- Value the abnormal gain in the process account = 20 × $24.50 = $490

Process 1 Account

	Units	$		Units	$
Materials	1,000	10,000	Transfers to process 2	980	24,010
Labour		8,000	Normal loss	40	480
Overheads		6,000			
Abnormal gain	20	490			
	1,000	24,490		1,000	24,490

- Transfer the abnormal gain to the abnormal loss/gain account at the process account value = 20 × $12 = $240
- Transfer the normal loss from the process account to the scrap account
- Transfer the abnormal gain from the abnormal loss/gain account at its scrap value = 20 × $12 = $240

Abnormal loss/gain account

	$		$
Scrap	240	Process 1 (AG)	490
Statement of profit or loss	250		
	490		490

Scrap account

	$		$
Process 1 (NL)	480	Abnormal loss/gain	240
		Cash (56 × $12)	240
	480		480

- Balance the abnormal loss/gain account and scrap account
- The balancing figure in the abnormal loss/gain account shows the net gain from having lost less than expected
- The balancing figure in the scrap account represents the cash received for the sale of the remaining loss

Suggested approach for answering normal loss, abnormal loss/gain questions

1. Calculate any normal loss units and value
2. Balance the units (input units = output units)
3. Calculate the net cost of inputs and expected output units
4. Calculate the average cost per unit:

$$\frac{\textbf{Net costs of input}}{\textbf{Expected output}}$$

5. Value the good output and abnormal loss or gain at this average cost per unit.
6. Transfer the abnormal loss or gain to the abnormal loss/gain account.
7. Transfer the normal loss to the scrap account (if any).
8. Transfer the abnormal loss or gain to the scrap account at the scrap value (if any).
9. Balance the abnormal loss/gain account and the scrap account.

Test your understanding 3

W&B Ltd produce a breakfast cereal that involves several processes. At each stage in the process, ingredients are added, until the final stage of production when the cereal is boxed up ready to be sold.

In Process 2, W&B Ltd have initiated a quality control inspection. This inspection takes place BEFORE any new ingredients are added in to Process 2. The inspection is expected to yield a normal loss of 5% of the input from Process 1. These losses are sold as animal fodder for $1 per kg.

The following information is for Process 2 for the period just ended:

	Units	$
Transfer from Process 1	500 kg	750
Material added in Process 2	300 kg	300
Labour	200 hrs	800
Overheads	–	500
Actual output	755 kg	–

Prepare the process account, abnormal loss and gain account, and scrap account for Process 2 for the period just ended.

5 Work-in-progress (WIP) and equivalent units (EUs)

Work in progress (WIP)

At the end of an accounting period there may be some units that have entered a production process but the process has not been completed. These units are called closing work in progress (CWIP) units.

- The output at the end of a period will consist of the following:
  - fully-processed units
  - part-processed units (CWIP).
- CWIP units become the Opening WIP (OWIP) units in the next accounting period.
- It would not be fair to allocate a full unit cost to part-processed units and so we need to use the concept of equivalent units (EUs) which shares out the process costs of a period fairly between the fully-processed and part processed units.

Concept of EUs

Process costs are allocated to units of production on the basis of EUs.

- The idea behind this concept is that a part-processed unit can be expressed as a proportion of a fully-completed unit.
- For example, if 100 units are exactly half-way through the production process, they are effectively equal to 50 fully-completed units. Therefore the 100 part-processed units can be regarded as being equivalent to 50 fully-completed units or 50 EUs.

Illustration 7 – CWIP and EUs

ABC Co has the following information for Process 1:

Period costs $4,440

Input 800 units

Output 600 fully -worked units and 200 units only 70% complete

There were no process losses.

Required:

Produce the process account

Solution:

Statement of equivalent units

	Physical units	% completion	EUs
Fully-worked units	600	100	600
CWIP	200	70	140
Total	800		740

Cost per EU = $4,440/740 units = $6 per equivalent unit

Process 1 Account

	Units	*$*		*Units*	*$*
Input	800	4,440	Transferred to next process (600 × $6)	600	3,600
			CWIP (140 EUs × $6)	200	840
	800	4,440		800	4,440

Different degrees of completion

For most processes the **material** is input at the **start** of the process, so it is only the addition of **labour** and **overheads** that will be **incomplete** at the end of the period.

- This means that the material cost should be spread over all units, but conversion costs (labour and overheads combined) should be spread over the EUs.
- This can be achieved using an expanded Statement of EUs which separates out the material, labour and overhead costs.

Illustration 8 – CWIP and EUs

For Process 1 in LJK Ltd the following is relevant for the latest period:

Material costs	500 units @ $8 per unit
Labour	$2,112
Overheads	150% of labour cost

Output: 400 fully-worked units, transferred to Process 2. 100 units only 40% complete with respect to conversion, but 100% complete with respect to materials.

There were no process losses.

Required:

Produce the process account.

Solution:

Statement of EUs

	Physical units	Materials		Conversion	
		%	EUs	%	EUs
Fully-worked units	400	100	400	100	400
CWIP	100	100	100	40	40
Total	500		500		440
Costs		Material	$4,000	Labour	$2,112
				Overheads	$3,168
Total costs			$4,000		$5,280
Cost per EU			$8		$12

The value of fully-worked units is 400 × ($8 + $12) **$8,000**

The value of CWIP is (100 × $8) + (40 × $12) **$1,280**

Process 1 Account

	Units	$		*Units*	$
Input	500	4,000	Transferred to process 2	400	8,000
Labour		2,112	CWIP	100	1,280
Overheads		3,168			
	500	9,280		500	9,280

Test your understanding 4

A firm operates a process costing system. Details of Process 2 for Period 1 are as follows.

During the period 8,250 units were received from the previous process at a value of $453,750, labour and overheads were $350,060 and material introduced was $24,750.

At the end of the period the closing WIP was 1,600 units which were 100% complete in respect of materials, and 60% complete in respect of labour and overheads. The balance of units was transferred to Finished goods.

There was no opening WIP or process losses.

Required:

Calculate the cost per EU, the value of finished goods and closing WIP.

Statement of EUs

	Physical units	Materials		Conversion	
		%	EUs	%	EUs
Fully-worked					
Closing WIP					
Total units					
Costs					
Total cost					
Cost per EU					

The value of finished goods is	$
The value of WIP is	$

6 Opening work in progress (OWIP)

If OWIP is present there are two methods that can be used to calculate the equivalent units and calculate the cost per equivalent unit:

- Weighted average method
- FIFO method.

Weighted average cost of production

- In the weighted average method no distinction is made between units in the process at the start of a period and those added during the period.
- Opening inventory costs are added to current costs to provide an overall average cost per unit.

- Imagine a bottle with some water in, when more water is added to the bottle it is not possible to tell which 'bit' of water was present as OWIP and what is 'new' water. The OWIP and material input into the process have mixed together.

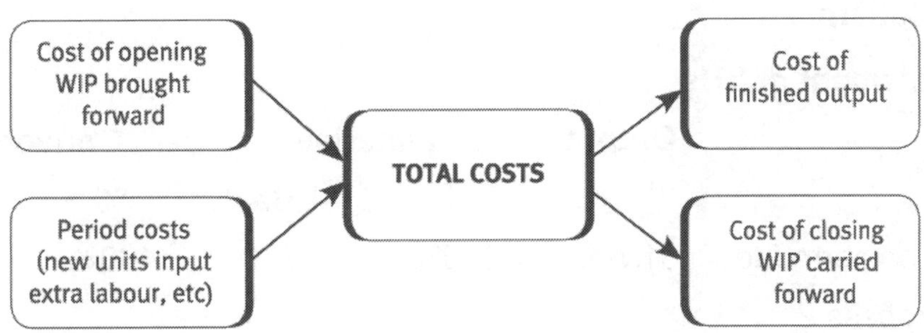

Illustration 9 – Weighted average cost of production

BR Ltd makes a product requiring several successive processes. Details of the first process for August are as follows:

Opening WIP:	400 units
Degree of completion:	
Materials (valued at $19,880)	100%
Conversion (valued at $3,799)	25%
Units transferred to Process 2	1,700 units
Closing WIP	300 units
Degree of completion:	
Materials	100%
Conversion	50%
Costs incurred in the period:	
Material	$100,000
Conversion	$86,000

There were no process losses.

Required:

Prepare the process account for August using the weighted average method.

Solution:

Statement of EUs

	Output	**Materials**		**Conversion**	
		%	**EUs**	**%**	**EUs**
Transferred to Process 2	1,700	100%	1,700	100%	1,700
CWIP	300	100%	300	50%	150
Total units	2,000		2,000		1,850
Costs:					
OWIP b/f cost			19,880		3,799
Period cost			100,000		86,000
Total cost			119,880		89,799
Cost per EU			$59.94		$48.54

Valuation of transfers to Process 2:

Materials = (1,700 × $59.94) = $101,898

Conversion = (1,700 × $48.54) = $82,518

Total = $184,416

Valuation of CWIP

Materials = (300 × $59.94) = $17,982

Conversion = (150 × $48.54) = $7,281

Total = $25,263

Process 1 Account

	Units	*$*		*Units*	*$*
OWIP	400	23,679	Transferred to Process 2	1,700	184,416
Materials	1,600	100,000	CWIP	300	25,263
Conversion		86,000			
	2,000	209,679		2,000	209,679

Test your understanding 5

A business makes one product that passes through a single process. The business uses the weighted average cost. The details of the process for the last period are as follows:

Materials	$98,000
Labour	$60,000
Production overheads	$39,000
Units added to the process	1,000

There were 200 units of opening WIP which are valued as follows:

Materials	$22,000
Labour	$6,960
Production overheads	$3,000

There were 300 units of closing WIP fully complete as to materials but only 60% complete for labour and 50% complete for overheads.

There were no process losses.

Calculate the following:

(a) The value of the completed output for the period.

(b) The value of the closing WIP.

FIFO cost of production

With the FIFO method it is assumed that the OWIP units need to be completed first before any more units can be started, for example cars on a production line. Therefore:

- completed output is made up of OWIP that has been finished in the period and units that have been made from beginning to end in the period
- if OWIP units are 75% complete with respect to materials and 40% complete with respect to labour, only 25% **more work** will need to be carried out with respect to materials and 60% with respect to labour
- the OWIP b/f costs are included in the final valuation of the completed units
- This means that the process costs in the period must be allocated between:
  - finishing the OWIP units
  - units started and completed in the period (fully-worked units)
  - CWIP units.

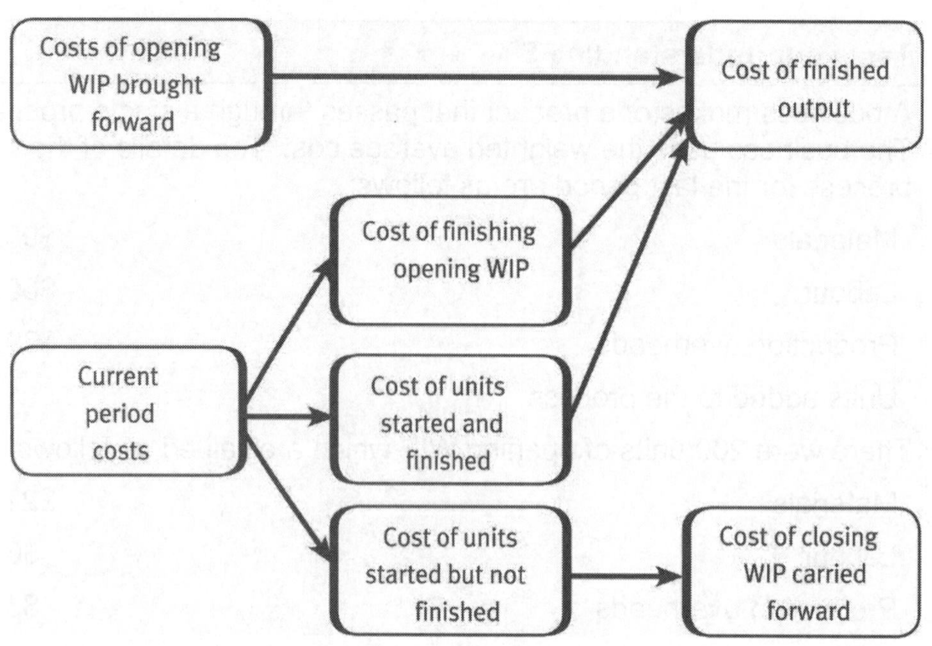

Illustration 10 – FIFO cost of production

BR Ltd makes a product requiring several successive processes. Details of the first process for August are as follows:

Opening WIP:	400 units
Degree of completion:	
Materials (valued at $19,880)	100%
Conversion (valued at $3,775)	25%
Units transferred to Process 2	1,700 units
Closing WIP	300 units
Degree of completion:	
Materials	100%
Conversion	50%
Costs incurred in the period:	
Material	$100,000
Conversion	$85,995

There were no process losses.

Required:

Prepare the process account for August using the FIFO method.

Solution:

Statement of EUs

	Physical units	Materials		Conversion	
		%	EUs	%	EUs
OWIP completed	400	0	0	75	300
Fully-worked in process	1,300	100	1,300	100	1,300
CWIP	300	100	300	50	150
Total	2,000		1,600		1,750
Costs			$100,000		$85,995
Cost per EU			$62.50		$49.14

Valuation of transfers to Process 2:

OWIP value from last period = $19,880 + $3,775 = $23,655

OWIP completed this period (conversion only) = 300 × $49.14 = $14,742

Fully-worked current period

Materials = 1,300 × $62.50 = $81,250

Conversion = 1,300 × $49.14 = $63,882

Total valuation of transfers to Process 2 = $183,529

Valuation of CWIP:

Materials = (300 × $62.50) = $18,750

Conversion = (150 × $49.14) = $7,371

Total valuation of CWIP = $26,121

Process 1 Account

	Units	$		*Units*	$
OWIP	400	23,655	Transferred to Process 2	1,700	183,529
Materials	1,600	100,000	CWIP	300	26,121
Conversion		85,995			
	2,000	209,650		2,000	209,650

Additional notes for solution to Illustration

Materials

Units completed in period	1,700
OWIP	(400)
Units completed from start to finished in the period	1,300

OWIP

The OWIP is 100% complete with respect to materials and therefore no further work or costs are involved in completing the opening WIP units.

The OWIP is 25% complete with respect to conversion costs and therefore 75% of the conversion work/costs are still outstanding.

Costs to complete OWIP and fully-worked units

Each unit started and finished in the period costs $(62.50 + 49.14) = $111.64

1,300 units were fully-worked in the process = 1,300 × $111.64 = $145,132

Costs to complete 400 units of OWIP = 300 units (conversion EUs) × $49.14 = $14,742

Costs to complete units transferred to Process 2

Cost of completing 1,700 units (1,300 fully-worked plus 400 OWIP) = $145,132 + $14,742 = $159,874

Total cost of units transferred to Process 2 = cost of completing 1,700 units plus costs already incurred in OWIP, i.e. $(19,880 + 3,775) = $23,655

Therefore, cost of 1,700 units transferred to Process 2 = $159,874 + $23,655 = $183,529

Test your understanding 6

AXL Ltd operates a process costing system. Details of Process 1 are as follows.

All materials used are added at the beginning of the process. Labour costs and production overhead costs are incurred evenly as the product goes through the process. Production overheads are absorbed at a rate of 100% of labour costs.

The following details are relevant to production in the period:

	Units	Materials	Labour and production overheads
Opening inventory	200	100% complete	75% complete
Closing inventory	100	100% complete	50% complete

Opening inventory

Costs associated with these opening units are $1,800 for materials. In addition $4,000 had been accumulated for labour and overhead costs.

Period costs

Costs incurred during the period were:

Materials	$19,000
Labour costs	$19,000

During the period, 2,000 units were passed to Process 2. There were no losses.

The company uses a FIFO method for valuing process costs.

Required:

Calculate the total value of the units transferred to Process 2.

7 Losses made part way through production

It is possible for losses or gains to be identified part way through a process. In such a case, EUs must be used to assess the extent to which costs were incurred at the time at which the loss/gain was identified.

Illustration 11 – Losses made part way through production

BLT manufactures chemicals and has a normal loss of 15% of material input. Information for February is as follows:

Material input 200 kg costing \$4.93 per kg

Labour and overheads \$4,100

Transfers to finished goods 160 kg

Losses are identified when the process is 40% complete

There is no opening or closing WIP.

Required:

Prepare the process account for February.

Solution:

- Calculate the normal loss units = 15% × 200 = 30 kg
- Balance the units (identify if there has been extra or less loss)

  Input units = Output units + Normal loss + Abnormal loss

  200 = 160 + 30 + 10
- Calculate the EUs for completed output plus the abnormal loss units. Normal loss is absorbed into good output so does not appear in the statement of EUs

Statement of EUs	**Total**	**EUs Materials**	**Conversion**
Finished units	160	160	160
Abnormal loss	10	10	4
Total EUs	170	170	164
Process costs		986	4,100
Cost per EU		\$5.80	\$25

Valuation of completed output

Total cost of completed unit =160EU × \$(5.80 + 25) = \$4,928

Valuation of abnormal loss

Abnormal loss = (10EU × \$5.80) + (4EU × \$25) = \$158

Process account

	Kg	$		Kg	$
Materials	200	986	Normal loss	30	–
Labour and overheads		4,100	Finished goods	160	4,928
			Abnormal loss	10	158
	200	5,086		200	5,086

Note: If an abnormal gain is identified then in the statement of equivalent units the abnormal gain units are deducted to calculate the total equivalent units.

8 Joint and by-products

The nature of process costing is such that processes often produce more than one product. These additional products may be described as either joint products or by-products. Essentially joint products are main products whereas by-products are incidental to the main products.

Joint products

Joint products are two or more products separated in the course of processing, each having a sufficiently **high saleable value** to merit recognition as a main product.

- Joint products include products produced as a result of the oil-refining process, for example, petrol and paraffin.
- Petrol and paraffin have similar sales values and are therefore equally important (joint) products.

By-products

By-products are outputs of **some value** produced incidentally in manufacturing something else (main products).

- By-products, such as sawdust and bark, are secondary products from the timber industry (where timber is the main or principal product from the process).
- Sawdust and bark have a relatively low sales value compared to the timber which is produced and are therefore classified as by-products.

Accounting treatment of joint products

The distinction between joint and by-products is important because the accounting treatment of joint products and by-products differs.

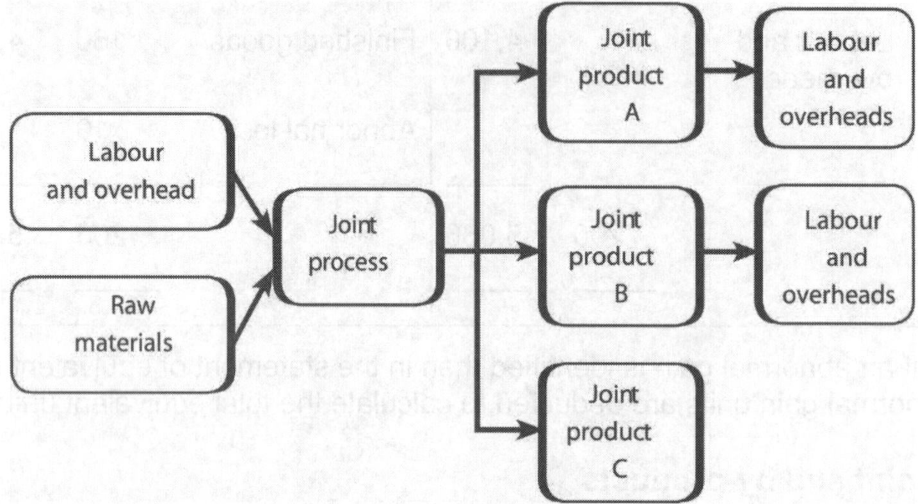

- Joint process costs occur before the split-off point. They are sometimes called pre-separation costs or common costs.
- The joint costs need to be apportioned between the joint products at the split-off point to obtain the cost of each of the products in order to value closing inventory and cost of sales.
- The basis of apportionment of joint costs to products is usually one of the following:
  - sales value of production (also known as market value)
  - production units
  - net realisable value.

Illustration 12 – Apportioning joint costs

Allison plc produces two products, X and Y, in a single joint process. Last month the joint costs were $75,000 when 10,000 units of Product X and 15,000 units of Product Y were produced. Additional processing costs were $15,000 for Product X and $10,000 for Product Y. Product X sells for $10, and Product Y sells for $5.

The joint cost allocations to Products X and Y using the **net realisable value** method would be:

Calculate the total net realisable value:

X: (10,000 units × $10) – $15,000 = $85,000

Y: (15,000 units × $5) – $10,000 = $65,000

Total net realisable value = $150,000

> Calculate the joint cost allocation:
>
> X: $75,000 ÷ $150,000 × $85,000 = $42,500
>
> Y:$75,000 ÷ $150,000 × $65,000 = $32,500
>
> The joint cost allocations to Products X and Y using the **physical units** method would be:
>
> X: $75,000 ÷ 25,000 units × 10,000 units = $30,000
>
> Y: $75,000 ÷ 25,000 units × 15,000 units = $45,000
>
> The joint cost allocations to Products X and Y using the **Market value** method would be:
>
> Calculate the total market value:
>
> X: 10,000 × $10 = $100,000
>
> Y: 15,000 × $5 = $75,000
>
> Total market value = $175,000
>
> Calculate the joint cost allocation:
>
> X: $75,000 ÷ 175,000 × $100,000 = $42,857
>
> Y: $75,000 ÷ 175,000 × $75,000 = $32,143

Accounting treatment of by-products

By-products are of less significance than the main products and may not require precise cost allocation. Factors that can influence the valuation and accounting treatment of by-products:

- Is the value of the by-product known at the time of production?
- Could the by-product be used in other production?
- Is the by-product an alternative to the main products?
- Is there a need for separate profit calculations for sales incentives or for control?

By-products can be accounted for using the following:

Non-cost methods

Non-cost methods make no attempt to allocate joint cost to the by-product but instead the proceeds either increase income or to reduce the cost of the main product.

- **Other income** – The net sales of by-products for the current period is recognised as other income and is reported in the income statement. This method is used where there is little value to the by-product, where any other method would be more expensive than the benefits received, or carrying by-products with the main products would not really affect the cost of the main product.
- **By-product revenue deducted from the main product(s) cost** – The net sales value of the by-products will be treated as a deduction from the cost of the main product(s). This is similar to the accounting treatment of normal loss. This is the most common method of accounting for by-product income.

Cost methods

Cost methods attempt to allocate some joint costs to by-products and to carry inventories at the allocated cost levels.

- **Replacement cost method** – values the by-product inventory at its opportunity cost of purchasing or replacing the by-products.
- **Total costs less by- products valued at standard price method** – By-products are valued at a standard price to avoid fluctuations in by-product value. This means that the main product cost will not be affected by any fluctuations in the by-product price. The standard price may be set arbitrarily, or it may reflect an average price over time. A variance account is used to account for the difference between actual and standard prices.
- **Joint cost pro-rata method** – allocates some of the joint cost to the by-product using any one of the joint cost allocation methods. This method is rarely used in practice.

Illustration 13 – Treatment of joint cost

Process M produces two joint products (A and B) and one by-product (C). Joint costs are apportioned on the basis of sales units.

The following information is relevant.

	Product A	Product B	Total
Sales units	2,000	8,000	10,000
Apportioned joint cost	$3,600	$14,400	$18,000

It is possible to sell by-product C after further processing for $0.50 per unit. The further processing costs are $0.20 per unit. 2,000 units of by-product C are produced.

Required:

If the by-product revenue is deducted from the main products cost how are the joint costs of $18,000 apportioned?

Solution:

Income from by-product = $(0.5 – 0.2) × 2,000 = $600

Joint costs are now $18,000 – $600 = $17,400

Total output units = 2,000 + 8,000 = 10,000 units

Joint cost allocated to Product A = $17,400 ÷ 10,000 units × 2,000 units = $3,480

Joint cost allocated to Product B = $17,400 ÷ 10,000 units × 8,000 units = $13,920

Test your understanding 7

A company operates a manufacturing process which produces joint products A and B, and by-product C.

Manufacturing costs for a period total $272,926, incurred in the manufacture of:

Product A 16,000 kg (selling price $6.10 per kg)

Product B 53,200 kg (selling price $7.50 per kg)

Product C 2,770 kg (selling price $1.20 per kg)

Product B requires further processing after separation from the other two products. This costs a total of $201,930.

Product C also requires further processing to make it saleable and this costs $0.40 per kg.

Required:

Calculate the total profit earned by Products A and B in the period, using the net realisable values (net income) to apportion joint costs. Assume that the by-product costs are deducted from the manufacturing costs.

Test your understanding 8

A company produces two products along with a single by-product. The joint process costs total $200,000. Product A can be sold for $450,000 after additional processing of $250,000; Product B can be sold for $600,000 after additional processing of $200,000. The by-product BP can be sold for $25,000 after packaging costs of $5,000. The by-product is accounted for using the by-product revenue deducted from the main product cost approach.

Required:

What would be the joint cost allocation using the net realisable value method?

	A	B
A	$60,000	$120,000
B	$66,667	$133,333
C	$77,143	$102,857
D	$85,714	$114,286

Test your understanding 9

Stone Mayson Inc is a manufacturer of granite slabs. Stone Mayson digs blocks of granite out of its quarry. All the granite extracted goes through the processes of quarrying and cutting. Two joint products (monuments and granite slabs) are produced along with a by-product called grit.

Monuments are cut, polished, and engraved in a variety of standard shapes, sizes, and patterns before being sold. The granite slabs are special-ordered by contractors for kitchen worktops. These slabs are cut and polished to exacting specifications. The small pieces of granite resulting from the cutting process are crushed and sold to farm-suppliers as poultry grit.

Stone Mayson has the following costs and output information:

Process	***Cost***	**Tonnes of output**
Quarry	$350,000	
Cutting	$250,000	
Monuments	$300,000	30,000
Granite slabs	$400,000	60,000
Grit	$10,000	5,000

A local farm-supplier purchases all of the grit that is produced at $40 per tonne. Assume that Stone Maysons uses the physical units method to allocate joint costs.

Required:

1 What would be the cost per tonne of monuments and granite slabs, assuming that the grit is accounted for as "Other Income"?

2 What would be the cost per tonne of monuments and granite slabs, assuming that the grit is accounted for as by-product revenue deducted from the main product cost?

9 Process accounts for joint and by-products

You may be required to deal with joint and by-products when preparing process accounts. Joint products should be treated as 'normal' output from a process. The treatment of by-products in process accounts is similar to the treatment of normal loss.

- The by-product income is credited to the process account and debited to a by-product account.
- To calculate the number of units in a period, by-product units (like normal loss) reduce the number of units output.
- When by-products are produced, the cost per unit is calculated as follows:

$$\frac{\textbf{Process costs (materials \& conversion costs) – Scrap value of normal loss – Sales value of by-product}}{\textbf{Expected number of units output (Input units – Normal loss units – By product units)}}$$

OR

$$\frac{\textbf{Net costs of inputs}}{\textbf{Expected output}}$$

10 Chapter summary

Joint and by-products

- Joint products are two or more products separated in processing, each having sufficiently high saleable value
- By-products are outputs of some value produced at the same time as joint products

Different types of production

Job costing

Form of specific order costing used when customer orders a specific job to be done. Each job is priced separately and is unique.

Batch costing

Form of specific order costing which is very similar to job costing. Each batch is a separately identifiable cost unit which is given a batch number.

Simple process costings

Costing method used when mass production of many identical products takes place, e.g. manufacture of bars of chocolate or cans of soup. All products manufactured are indistinguishable from each other and so an average cost per unit is calculated for each process.

Process costing with gains and losses

- Normal loss = expected loss. Value is $0 unless it has a scrap value.
- Abnormal loss is extra unexpected loss.
- Abnormal gain occurs when actual loss is less than expected.
- Abnormal loss and gain are valued at same value as good output.

Process costing with opening WIP

Weighted average method does not distinguish between opening WIP units and units added in process. FIFO method distinguishes between opening WIP, units started and finished in process ('fully- worked' units) and closing WIP.

Process costing with WIP and EUs

Not fair to allocate full unit cost to a part-processed unit. Idea behind the concept of EUs is that a part-processed unit can be expressed as a proportion of a fully-completed unit.

Process costs are allocated to units in a process on the basis of EUs.

Test your understanding answers

Test your understanding 1

C

Job costing is customer-driven with customers ordering a specific job to be done. It is also possible for production to be completed within a single accounting period.

Test your understanding 2

	$
Direct materials 50 kg × $4	200
Direct labour 30 hours × $9	270
Variable production overhead 30 × $6	180
Fixed overheads $80,000/20,000 × 30	120
Other overheads	40
Total cost	810

Test your understanding 3

Process 2 Account

	Kg	$		Kg	$
Transfer from Process 1	500	750	Finished goods	755	2,265
Additional materials	300	300	Normal loss	25	25
Labour		800	Abnormal loss	20	60
Overheads		500			
	800	2,350		800	2,350

Normal loss = 5% of transfer from Process 1 = 500 kg × 0.05 = 25 kg
Scrap value of normal loss = 25 kg × $1 = $25
Cost per unit = ($2,350 – $25)/(800 kg – 25 kg) = $3

Abnormal gains and losses account

	$		$
Process 2	60	Scrap (20 × $1)	20
		Statement of profit or loss	40
	60		60

Scrap account

	$		$
Process 2 (normal loss)	25	Cash (45 × $1)	45
Abnormal gain and loss	20		
	45		45

Test your understanding 4

	Physical units	Materials		Conversion	
		%	EUs	%	EUs
Fully-worked	6,650	100	6,650	100	6,650
CWIP	1,600	100	1,600	60	960
Total units			8,250		7,610
Costs:			$453,750		$350,060
			$24,750		
Total cost			$478,500		$350,060
Cost per EU			$58		$46

The value of finished goods is (W1)	$691,600
The value of CWIP is (W2)	$136,960

Workings

(W1)	Value of finished goods		
	Materials: 6,650 × $58	=	$385,700
	Conversion: 6,650 × $46	=	$305,900
	Total	=	$691,600
(W2)	Value of CWIP		
	Materials: 1,600 × $58	=	$92,800
	Conversion: 960 × $46	=	$44,160
	Total	=	$136,960

Test your understanding 5

Statement of EUs

	Materials		Labour		Overheads	
	%	EU	%	EU	%	EU
Output	100	900	100	900	100	900
CWIP	100	300	60	180	50	150
Total EUs		1,200		1,080		1,050

	$	$	$
Costs – **period**	98,000	60,000	39,000
OWIP	22,000	6,960	3,000
Total costs	120,000	66,960	42,000
Cost per unit	$100	$62	$40

(Total costs/total EUs)

(a) Value of completed output = 900 × $(100 + 62 + 40) = $181,800

(b)

Materials	300 × $100	30,000
Labour	180 × $62	11,160
Overheads	150 × $40	6,000
Value of CWIP		47,160

Test your understanding 6

Statement of EUs

	Output	Materials		Conversion	
		%	EUS	%	EUS
OWIP completed	200	0	0	25	50
Fully-worked in process	1,800	100	1,800	100	1,800
CWIP	100	100	100	50	50
Total	2,100		1,900		1,900
Costs			$19,000		$19,000 + $19,000*= $38,000
Cost per EU			$10		$20

* Overheads are absorbed at 100% of labour cost.

Value of units passed to Process 2:

OWIP value from last period	= $1,800 + $4,000	= $5,800
OWIP completed this period:		
Conversion only	= 50 × $20	= $1,000
Fully-worked current period		
Materials	= 1,800 × $10	= $18,000
Conversion	= 1,800 × $20	= $36,000
Total = $54,000		

Total value of units transferred to Process 2 = $60,800

Test your understanding 7

Net revenue from product C = $(1.2 – 0.4) = $0.80

Costs to apportion = Joint process costs – net revenue from product C
= $272,926 – (2,770 kg × $0.80)
= $270,710

Net realisable value (16,000 kg × $6.10) + [(53,200 kg × $7.50) – $201,930] = $97,600 + $197,070 = $294,670

Joint cost apportioned to A = $270,710 ÷ $294,670 × $97,600 = $89,664

Joint cost apportioned to B = $270,710 ÷ $294,670 × $197,070 = $181,046

Profit from A = $97,600 – $89,664 = $7,936

Profit from B = $197,070 – $181,046 = $16,024

Total profit = **$23,960**

Test your understanding 8

A

Adjusted joint cost after reduction of net sale of by-product = $200,000 – ($25,000 – $5,000) = $180,000

Joint cost allocation ratios are computed using the net realisable value method as follows:

A: $450,000 – $250,000 = $200,000

B: $600,000 – $200,000 = $400,000

Total net realisable value = $600,000

Joint cost allocation is computed as follows:

A: $180,000 ÷ $600,000 × $200,000 = $60,000

B: $180,000 ÷ $600,000 × $400,000 = $120,000

Test your understanding 9

1 Grit accounted for as "Other Income":

Joint cost to be allocated = $350,000 Quarry + $250,000 Cutting = $600,000

Total units = 30,000 tons + 60,000 tons = 90,000 tonnes

Joint cost allocated to Monument = $600,000 ÷ 90,000 tonnes × 30,000 tonnes = $200,000

Joint cost allocated to Slabs = $600,000 ÷ 90,000 tonnes × 60,000 tonnes = $400,000

Total cost for Monument = $200,000 + $300,000 = $500,000

Cost per tonne for Monument = $500,000 ÷ 30,000 tonnes = **$16.67 per tonne**

Total cost for Slabs = $400,000 + $400,000 = $800,000

Cost per tonne for Slabs = $800,000 ÷ 60,000 tonnes = **$13.33 per tonne**

2 Grit accounted for as by-product revenue deducted from main product cost:

Sales of grit (5,000 tonnes × $40) = $200,000

Less: Separable costs of processing = $10,000

Net realisable value = $190,000

Joint cost to be allocated = $350,000 Quarry + $250,000 Cutting – $190,000 By-product net sales = $410,000

Total units = 30,000 tons + 60,000 tons = 90,000 tonnes

Joint cost allocated to Monument = $410,000 ÷ 90,000 tonnes × 30,000 tonnes = $136,667

Joint cost allocated to Slabs = $410,000 ÷ 90,000 tonnes × 60,000 tonnes = $273,333

Total cost for Monument = $136,667 + $300,000 = $436,667

Cost per tonne for Monument = $436,667 ÷ 30,000 tonnes = **$14.56 per tonne**

Total cost for Slabs = $273,333 + $400,000 = $673,333

Cost per tonne for Slabs = $673,333 ÷ 60,000 tonnes = **$11.22 per tonne**

Chapter

8

Service and operation costing

Chapter learning objectives

Upon completion of this chapter you will be able to:

- identify situations where the use of service/operation costing is appropriate
- illustrate suitable unit cost measures that may be used in different service/operation situations
- carry out service cost analysis in simple service industry situations.

PER

One of the PER performance objectives (PO12) is to apply different management accounting techniques is different business contexts to effectively manage and use resources. Working through this chapter should help you understand how to demonstrate that objective.

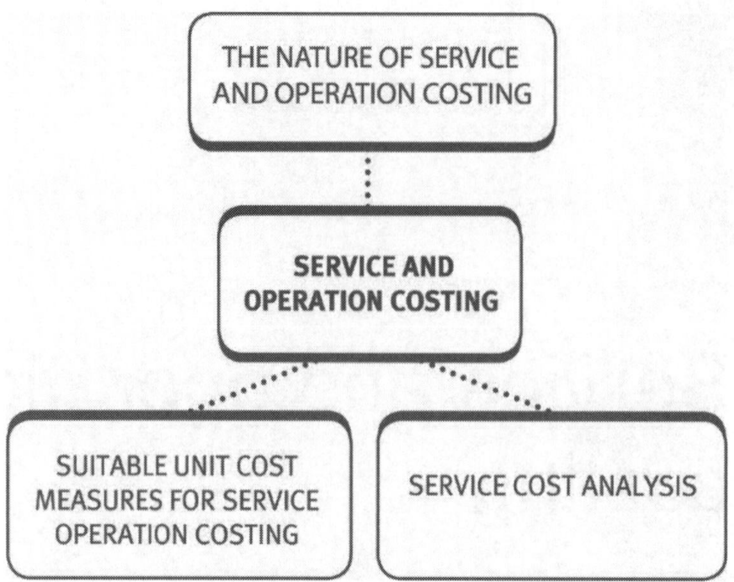

1 The nature of service and operation costing

Service costing

Service costing is used when an organisation or department provides a service, such as an accountancy firm preparing the accounts for a company.

There are four main differences between the 'output' of service industries and the products of manufacturing industries.

- **Intangibility** – output is in the form of 'performance' rather than tangible ('touchable') goods.
- **Heterogeneity** – the nature and standard of the service will be variable due to the high human input.
- **Simultaneous production and consumption** – the service that you require cannot be inspected in advance of receiving it.
- **Perishability** – the services that you require cannot be stored.